Any Kid
Can Be A Super Star

Maureen G. Mulvaney

Practical Attitude Technologies for Real Parents
TO RAISE A SUPER STAR KID!
*(A Super Star Kid is any child who is Healthy, Happy,
Self-Assured, Bright, Kind-Hearted, Loving, and "Bonker's Free")*

Dedication

To Marie and Paul Mulvaney, two of the most gifted parents in this universe. Thank you for your understanding, encouragement and consistency. You made growing up fun, loving, safe, and truly wondrous. The wee angels blessed me when they let me be born into the Mulvaney family. You helped us all become SUPER STARS!

Thank You

Thank you Oprah, you encouraged self-help books and Americans began to read.

Thank you Rosie O'Donnel, you encouraged parenting and Americans saw the joy in having kids.

Thank you Hillary Clinton, you encouraged community and Americans discovered it does take a village to raise a child.

Acknowledgments

Thank you Marie P. Mulvaney, for being a Super Star MOM. You motivated me, encouraged me, and gave me the inspiration to write this book.

Thank you Mayre G. Mulvaney, little MGM, for being a Super Star daughter. I searched the world over and God sent me you. You warm my heart and tickle my soul. You will always be a Super Star to me.

Thank you Susan Mulvaney, for being a Super Star sister. You have always been there for me and I appreciate you more than you will every know.

Thank you Paul Wayne Mulvaney, for being a Super Star brother. You make me laugh.

Thank you Yvonne O. Pena, for being my Super Star assistant. You took care of all the details so I could write this book.

Thank you Nancy Lieberman-Cline for being a Super Star role model. You opened the doors for the rest of us to skip through.

Thank you Heidi Grimes, Shirin Bhaloo, Eleanor Jordan, and Carol Elias for being Super Star teachers. You believed any kid could be a Super Star, and all the children you touch become Super Stars.

Thank you Carla Bruce for being a Super Star editor. You accepted the challenge and made an impossible deadline come to pass. Your attentive eyes, nimble hands, and skillful typesetting created a masterful interior design.

Thank you Hannah Reiter for being a Super Star artist and designing the perfect cover.

Thank you all my family members, friends, neighbors, "bus group," students, and clients who shared their stories.

Thank you all my past and present Master Mind partners (Trish Adams, Sharon Bacher, Ann Bitters, Shari Christie, Marilyn Chileen, Susan Marchese, and Esther Slater) for helping me stay on the divine higher path.

Contents

Introduction

Like most parents today, I have a very hectic lifestyle and wear many different hats. As a single mom, I support my family and make my income as an International Professional Speaker and an Arbonne distributor. I travel the world speaking to various Fortune 500 companies, healthcare, educational and women's organizations. My most popular title is: **"Attitude Technologies for the New Millennium"** or better known as **"How to Keep from Going Bonkers."**

I help participants view change as a positive force for innovation in the New Millennium! I get paid to have fun. It's not a "real" job by some people's standard, but God help me, I love it! My Arbonne business allows me to help children and adults feel great and maintain healthy lifestyles!

Although I enjoy speaking and Arbonne, my real life's profession is being a parent! My goal is to raise a SUPER STAR KID! A Super Star Kid, by my definition, is any child who is

Healthy, Happy, Self-Assured, Bright,
Kind-Hearted, Loving, and "Bonker's Free"!

I was in my forties before I adopted my daughter, Mayre G. Mulvaney—love of my life. Knowing that a healthy, happy, self-assured, bright, kind-hearted, loving, "Bonker's Free" SUPER STAR does not just appear at age 18, I started working with Mayre from day one.

Although Mayre was adopted, at age one and one-half, from an orphanage in Vietnam, I gave birth to her through my heart. We bonded instantly. Mayre was malnourished, did not speak, had respiratory disease, a gaping cleft palate, and hearing loss. Many professionals told me not to expect very much from this child. *She will probably be delayed in speech, language and all subjects.*

Thank Heaven, I didn't listen! By age three, Mayre was reading on a first grade level, by kindergarten she had won a Bronze Medal in an Arizona State University Essay Contest, and in first grade she won the Gold Medal (over 1000 children submitted essays). In second grade, Mayre, one of the youngest participants, performed her original piano composition at the Junior Original Competition in San Antonio, Texas.

Friends, neighbors and teachers were astonished at the way I was raising Mayre. They plagued me with questions. They wanted me to write a book about how I taught a child from a Vietnamese orphanage to a be Super Star by age three.

"Write a book . . . Are you crazy . . . I don't even have the time to do the laundry" was my reply. "You don't understand! I'm a 'wash and wear' single mom who is constantly on the run. When do you think I would have the time to write a book?"

Then it dawned on me, I would write the book the same way I do everything else, with great flexibility and creativity. I would get up earlier, speak into a tape recorder while on the run, and ask my family and friends to help. Before I knew it, I had begun to jot down practical ideas and techniques. The stories just flowed from me; remember, I am a speaker by trade and Irish by birth—the blarney is inherited!

Of course, I could make it one of those books with a zillion studies and charts that no one would ever read. After all, I do have a B.A. in Special Education and Elementary Education plus a Master's Degree from Boston University in Counseling Psychology. I taught college Psychology for years and know how to be academic and boring, when I choose. But I remembered my 15 years of teaching elementary school.

My goal was to instill in my students a joy of learning. As a teacher, I delivered information in a humorous, easy-to-understand, interactive manner. I wanted my students to remember and use the information immediately in their lives.

My goal, for this book, is the same—to deliver practical information that you, as a parent, can use immediately. I want you to have a "Strategic Plan for Parenting a Super Star Child." I finally wrote this book because, like you, I'm an overworked, sleep-deprived, parent. I desperately needed and wanted someone to give me a PLAN to get through this thing called *parenting*. But when I researched other parenting books, they gave information about parenting but no step-by-step plan.

This book will give you an easy-to-understand practical, FUN Strategic PLAN to Parent!

Please use this book! Forget what your elementary teachers said, "DO NOT WRITE IN YOUR BOOK!" Mark this book up as if it were the Yellow Pages. Commit to doing the exercises. Add your own stories, tidbits, and practical ideas, or e-mail your thoughts and ideas to me and I'll gladly include them in the next edition.

When you have completed the exercises, pass it along to family and friends. I don't care how you get the information in use or who gets the credit—just use the ideas to raise Healthy, Happy, Self-Assured, Bright, Kind-Hearted, Loving, "Bonker's Free" SUPER STARS. Enjoy!

Note

☆ Throughout this book I mention God. If God is not your *higher power*, please substitute your higher power's name instead.

☆ I am a single Irish mother with an adopted Vietnamese child. In the past, our family would have been called non-traditional. Nowadays, we're just called a family! That's right, only 25% of families in America have a mom, dad, 2.5 children, and a dog!

Whenever I refer to parent or parents, please know it includes whatever kind of parent: mom or dad single parent, traditional married mother and father parents, mother and mother parents, father and father parents, step-parents, biological parent, adoptive parent, love-partner parents, grandparents or whatever combination thereof. This book is meant to be inclusive—not exclusive.

Mom and Mayre (age 2 1/2) celebrate coming to America!.

Part One

Attitude
Technologies

Some of the attitudes you now hold about parenting are antiquated and ineffective.

Attitude Technologies are new and improved attitudes for Parents of Super Stars.

☆ Enjoy the Ride

Stop watching TV and start watching the commercials. Yes, you read that correctly, watch the commercials. You can learn so much more from the commercials than you can from the TV shows. For instance, not long ago, there was a Nissan commercial showing a Japanese man holding several dogs. The commercial said, *Dogs love trucks . . . Enjoy the ride.*

Well honey, I am a baby-boomer and I don't get half of the commercials on TV today. I had no idea what the Nissan commercial meant. So, I went down the street to visit one of the Generation X kids and asked, "Could you explain that commercial to me."

The girl looked at me and said, "Duh . . . well MGM . . . It is like this—like it means—like . . . ENJOY THE RIDE—like . . . duh . . . ENJOY RIGHT NOW . . . like . . . ENJOY THE MOMENT!" Then I had to get someone else to explain that to me. Finally, I got it—ENJOY THE MOMENT.

As baby boomers, we did not learn to enjoy anything. We delayed gratification. We believed:

I will enjoy my life when I graduate from college.

I will enjoy my life when I get the new job.

I will enjoy my life when I get married.

I will enjoy my life when I have children.

3

I will enjoy my life when I get a new house.

I will enjoy my life when I get a new spouse.

It's endless. Our attitude seems to be: I will enjoy WHEN . . . my children are perfect, when my spouse is perfect, when my job is perfect, or when my life is perfect.

HELLO! If you are waiting till every thing is perfect before you start enjoying being a parent, you will be in

Maureen, I LOVE BEING MOM!

heaven first. Angels are the only creatures I know of who are perfect; the rest of us on earth are striving to be effective and to be the best we can be. Perfection rarely exists on earth. Stop waiting until everything is exactly the way you want it to be. We, parents, are still trying to be the Perfect Parent, the Perfect Employee, the Perfect Boss, the Perfect Mate . . . the Perfect Everything. Therefore, we can not enjoy just being mamma or daddy.

ENJOY BEING A PARENT

To be an effective parent, you must first enjoy being a parent. There are no perfect parents (even though some look that way from the outside). **Parents make mistakes. Parents have good days and not so good days.** (Hopefully, this book will help you have more good days than bad ones.)

Stop trying to be the perfect parent. **Start enjoying each stage of your child.** I've heard parents say, "I can't wait to get through the *Terrible Twos* with my child." First, change your attitude to the *Terrific Twos*, then start enjoying those Terrific Twos. Those precious moments only last a nano-second. Once they are gone, you cannot get them back.

Now, some of you are beginning to feel guilty like the mother who recently called me. She said, "I feel so bad, I didn't do all the things you did with your little one. I wasn't a very good mother." I told her feeling guilty would not help her to be a better parent or help her enjoy her children now, even though they were grown. When you feel guilty, you figure guilt is punishment enough. Then you go right out and do the same thing over and over.

Stop Feeling Guilty and Start Enjoying!

Wouldn't it be better to tell yourself, "My parenting skills, back then, were not the most effective. I will go to each of my children and apologize. I will ask them for their help to be a more effective parent now."

Please know that, most of the time, you can correct the parenting mistakes you have made in the past. No matter what age your children are now, you can go to them and start over. Of course, you cannot start over using the same old skills—you must learn new skills and new attitudes. You can start right this very minute to do things differently, and your children will react differently.

☆ Love leads the way
☆ Patience is the key
☆ New Attitudes and Skills open the door

Enjoy the challenges of raising children because they will make you laugh later on in life. Enjoy each moment instead of waiting for the *perfect moment*. I don't have many perfect moments, but I do have laundry moments, race-to-the-store moments, and shopping moments. Instead of waiting for the perfect moment to talk to the kids, talk to them while doing the laundry, feeding the fish, driving in the car, and getting the groceries. Don't wait for the perfect moment to set aside "Talk Time" with your children—talk as you go. Enjoy, Enjoy, Enjoy!

Attitude Technologies
ENJOY THE RIDE . . . ENJOY BEING A PARENT

1. Stop feeling guilty. Guilt gives you an excuse to stay the same.
2. Stop trying to be perfect and strive to be effective.
3. Enjoy the ride. Parenting is a wonderful adventure.

   Love leads the way, Patience is the key, and New Attitudes and Skills open the door to the adventure of parenting.
4. ENJOY BEING A PARENT!

Insights and Notes

2

☆ Parental Modeling

Parental modeling is ever so important. You can forget that old saying: *Do as I say not as I do.* **Children will do what you do!** You are the leader. By the very fact that you chose to have children, you must take the lead.

When I taught elementary school, Fridays were difficult. It seemed like my students always lost their minds on Fridays. Of course, I blamed the student for misbehaving. Then, one week, I was off on Wednesday and Thursday. When I returned on Friday, my students were fine. Instead of blaming, I began to look at my own behavior. I discovered by the time Friday rolled around, I was exhausted. I had expended tons of energy all week and I was just plain tired on Friday. I was less patient, less understanding, and more demanding. My students sensed this and reacted in kind. Actually, they mirrored my behavior. Oops!!!

Have you ever gone to the store and the check-out person was not in a particularly good mood? Did the checker have to come out and say, "I hate this job, I hate this check-out register, and I hate these long lines"? Or did you just know it? I think you just knew it. How did you react? Most of us react in kind, meaning we react the way we are treated. We mirror the behavior that we see. Oops!!!

Have you ever had acquaintances you liked but you were really turned off by them because they were too talkative,

Marie P. Mulvaney modeled positive attitudes and skills for Maureen, who is repeating the pattern for Mayre.

selfish, impolite, rash, or messy? Maybe they were just mirroring the parts of you that you are still working to improve.

Our children mirror our vulnerabilities. They hit us right in our weak spots and they don't even know they are doing it. When I chose to adopt Mayre, I made a conscientious decision to spend as much time with her as I could. I decided something had to give if I were to have more time. Housework seemed like the best choice, so I just gave it up. As my friend, Rita Davenport says, "You can eat right off my floors because there is the mustard and the ketchup . . . ." It was my choice to give up housework.

Although I am totally organized, I dislike the fact that I am now messy. So the other day, Mayre and I were racing around the house trying to find Mayre's shoes for school. I heard these words come out of my mouth: "If you just kept your shoes all together in your closet, in a neat and organized fashion, we would not have to search for your shoes on a daily basis." Before I had even finished the sentence, I looked around the room and saw three pairs of my own shoes strewn about the room. Where or where could Mayre have learned this behavior? Oops!!!

TAKE RESPONSIBILITY

Take personal responsibility to model the behaviors you want your children to have.

If you want polite children . . . then you must be polite.

If you want children to awaken in a pleasant mood . . . then you must awaken pleasantly.

If you want neat children . . . then you must be neat.

If you want happy children . . . then you must be happy.

If you want physically fit children . . . then you must be physically fit.

If you want financially responsible children . . . then you must be financially responsible.

MODEL HONEST BEHAVIOR

My father valued honesty and modeled it in all his behaviors. Notice I said HE MODELED HONEST BEHAVIORS IN ALL HIS BEHAVIORS. I have observed some parents using the words, "Be honest," then their behavior showed the opposite as they cheated on their taxes or didn't pay their full share. The loophole was always, "Everyone does it."

My father's words and actions were congruent. When we were young, Dad took my mother and all three children to the fair. When we got to the toll-booth, the woman only charged my father for one of the children. It was an oversight on her part. My father quickly said, "Madam, all three of my children should pay as they are over six."

The woman responded, "That's a first. Most people would have paid for just one child and said nothing."

My father said, "Then my children would have lost a valuable lesson in honesty."

Another time when we lived in New York, my dad bought some tiles to replace the kitchen floor. When he got home from the store, he discovered the man made a huge error in my father's favor. Dad collected all of us children and drove us back to the store to show the man his error. The man did not believe my father and insisted there was no error until my father redid the math for him. The man was floored (get it . . . tiles . . . floored, okay, some of these I do just for me!). He thanked my father and sent him a wonderful letter that my father cherished.

☆ Dad valued honesty
☆ He talked about honesty
☆ He modeled honesty
☆ We learned and valued honesty too

Send Congruent Messages

I see so many parents who want their children to have their values but teach them the exact opposite. I recently sat next to a doctor on the plane. He was complaining about his son and daughter. He said they did not appreciate anything. He and his family had just returned from a very expensive vacation yet no one had any fun because they were bored.

I asked the doctor, "How did you get to be the person you are today?"

He replied, "It was all my hard work and tough experiences that got me here."

Then I asked, "Did your children have to work to earn the money to go on the vacation?"

He looked at me like I had lost my mind and said, "Of course not. I was poor as a kid. I don't want my children to have to go through what I went through. I want them to have everything I never had!"

What's wrong with this picture? ... DUH ... The doctor valued hard work. The doctor valued setting goals and working toward those goals. The doctor obviously was unaware of his own values because he turned around and taught his children, through his own modeling, the exact opposite of what he wanted for them. He taught them:

You can have anything you want. You do not have to work for it because I will give it to you.

To get what you want, all you have to do is ask—better yet, please whine or behave like a "brat" and I will give it to you faster.

The doctor used words to tell his children to work hard, but his actions (modeling) sent the exact opposite message. The children did not even hear the words because his actions spoke so loudly: **You do not have to work at all for anything. Just exist and I will give you whatever you desire!**

1. Be aware of your modeling (actions)

Your children's behaviors will give you the answer as to whether you are effectively modeling or if you need to make a change.

Ask yourself honestly, "Do I do that?" (Look at your own behaviors).

Do I say one thing and do something else? (Are your words and actions congruent?)

2. Observe your own behavior

Make a decision to either change your behavior or accept your behavior. If you will change your own behavior, I guarantee that your children will follow your lead (with a little time and patience). If you decide to accept your behavior, then be aware that your children will stay the same, as well. Don't forget to accept their behavior when you accept your own.

3. Observe your own words and modeling (actions)

Do you say, "Pick up your toys," then leave your briefcase and mail strewn about the room? Do you say, "Show me respect," and then yell, "Get over here NOW"? Do you say, "Don't hit your brother," then whack him for hitting his brother?

4. Make sure your words and modeling (actions) match

If you ask your child to pick up his toys, please put your stuff in a certain place every day as well. If you ask your child for respect, then please use the magic words every time with him. If you ask your child not to use violence, then please do use violence with him. Use words instead.

5. Flip the stop switch on guilt

Lest you turn on the guilt machine again, believing all your child's unwanted behavior flows from you, flip the stop switch before you flip guilt into high gear. Not all your children's behaviors comes from you. As they grow, teachers, peers, friends, and many others will influence them. Great parental modeling does not insure that someone else will never unduly influence your children. But it does give them a rock solid foundation upon which to build their SUPER STAR life.

Attitude Technologies
PARENTAL MODELING

1. You are the LEADER.
2. Children will do WHAT YOU DO not what you say.
3. Children often mirror the parent's behavior.
4. If your children display behaviors you do not like, look at your behaviors and modeling.
5. Change your own behavior or accept it. Then accept it in your children.
6. Choose the behavior you will model. Match your words and actions.

Insights and Notes

3

 Change Your
Attitudes and
Change Your Life

To be a teacher, I had to go to college for four years. To get a driver's license, I had to go to driver's education for a semester. To get a Master's Degree to become a Psychologist, I had to go back to college for two more years. When I got a speeding ticket, I had to go to remedial driving class for a weekend. **Yet, for the most important job of my life . . . being a parent . . . I did not have to go to school!**

LEARN TO BE A PARENT

I wondered, *Where do you learn to be a parent?* I asked friends and clients, "Where did you go to school to be a parent?"

Most laughed and responded: "You don't need to go to school to be a parent, you just have a kid," or "I don't know where I learned to be a parent, it's just who I am."

It seems most parents believe they are somehow born genetically equipped with a "parenting chip." This "parenting chip" evidently kicks in when a child is born or adopted.

Once that child appears . . . WHA-LA! . . . You are now a parent with a parenting database! WRONG!!!

This book is not for parents who think they are genetically pre-disposed to be parents. This book is for REAL PARENTS who are willing to do the exercises and work it takes to become EFFECTIVE PARENTS. This book is for parents who are willing to change their attitude **from** *Parenting is something that just happens to you* **to** *Parenting is a role I choose . . . I will be the best parent I can be. I will do what is necessary to be the best parent I can be.* When your attitude changes, your behaviors will change also. It would be hard to gain new information about parenting and still use all the same behaviors. **Change your attitude and you will change your behavior!**

The parenting skills that you either possess or do not possess are not genetic in nature; but they are what you have learned along the way to becoming an adult. You watched and experienced your own parents, teachers, family friends, and relatives, and you picked up certain attitudes that drive your behaviors.

Spaced Repetition

Spaced repetition is how we learn many of our attitudes.

For example: If I say "Plop Plop" what comes to mind?

The Alka Seltzer commercial . . . Plop Plop Fizz Fizz, Oh what a relief it is.

> **If you see it, hear it, or experience it 6 times a day for 21 days, you own it!**

Although that commercial has not been on for almost 25 years, you remembered it as if it were yesterday. WHY? Because it painlessly went into your human computer.

Our human computer runs day and night. We take in everything we see, hear and experience. Like a video camera that is left on record for six hours, we take it all in. There is no editing, the video is just running. Later, when and if we choose, we adults edit the tape. Most children never edit. They just take it all in. In my opinion, that is how we learn our attitudes and beliefs about everything in life.

If you saw, heard, or experienced your PARENTS:	You developed the ATTITUDE:
Praise and encourage you	It was all right to take risks and try new things
Criticize and discourage you	It was not okay to make mistakes
Invite friends and family to your house	People are basically good and can be trusted
Not invite people to the house and had no friends	People are basically bad and cannot be trusted
Laugh and enjoy life	Life is enjoyable and can be fun
Frown and dislike everything	Life is a struggle and must be hard

Most of the attitudes you hold about life are not even yours. They came from parents, teachers, friends, relatives, preachers and priests. Some of these attitudes have worked and served you well, but many of these attitudes have not worked, and the only reason you keep using them is that they are COMFORTABLE.

For example, if I asked you to say something nice about yourself, could you do it? Most of us would find this very difficult to do because as children we heard from many sources, "Don't be conceited" or "Be humble." We began to believe that saying nice things about ourselves was conceited and we should not do it.

If you are a woman, you probably even took it a step further and made self-depreciating statements when someone gave you a complement. "MGM, that is an attractive outfit." My reply used to be, "This old thing, I got it at the Salvation Army." Now I simply say, "Thank you."

This belief might have served you well in Ms. O'Leary's third grade class, but as an adult it just does not work. Throughout this book, I will be asking you to say nice things to your children and love-partners. How will you be able to do that if you won't even say something nice about yourself?

This little angel could change anyone's attitudes. Mayre is a Super Star.

You cannot give away what you do not have. If you do not have nice things to say about yourself, you won't say nice things about other people—even your children. Then to ensure the other person does not become conceited, you give a compliment and put a zinger at the end so it hurts when it goes in. Oops!!!

> **Some people would rather die than give up a belief that just does not work.**

Just because millions of people hold a particular belief or attitude about something does not mean it is effective. Communism is dead. It did not work. I have been to Cambodia, Vietnam, China and Russia and I have seen, first hand, that it does not work. Yet people would rather starve in the streets of Moscow than to give up a belief that does not work. That is how strong attitudes can be.

Holding on to the attitudes you now possess will continue to get you the same results. Do you really want that?

I hope you want to change your attitudes so you can change your behaviors.

HOW DO YOU CHANGE ATTITUDES?

REMEMBER: Changing your attitude about parenting will precipitate changing your behaviors.

1. Become Uncomfortable

Although most human beings thrive on a new challenge, once we are on the job, in the marriage, or in the relationship, we almost automatically begin to look for ways to become comfortable.

Comfort can kill a marriage. *At the beginning,* you dated each other. You were on your best behavior. You felt challenged and it felt great. Then you married. At first you were still on your best behavior. But one day you decided: *I've been good long enough. It's time to be myself and let it all hang out.* And you did, literally. You aimed to be comfortable. The good news about Comfort is it brings pleasure. The bad news about Comfort is it also brings boredom.

> **Give up old parenting attitudes that no longer work.**
>
> **Embrace new attitude technologies that will work for you and your family!**

Once people become bored they stop doing the little things that attracted them in the first place, like talking to each other. They start to wander, thinking the grass is greener somewhere else. BAM . . . the marriage is in trouble because they were just so very comfortable. We usually only make changes in our marriage, or in life, when things get uncomfortable. It is okay to be uncomfortable. It is challenging and exciting.

Think about it—unless you love learning and are truly enlightened, the only reason you are reading this book is because you are in need of answers to help you on your parenting journey. You are uncomfortable with parts of your parenting style. Things have gotten a little out of control and you need help.

Give up parenting attitudes that do not work—attitudes like the following:

I will be a great parent just because I love children.

Having a child makes me a parent.

No training or school is necessary to become a parent!

Make your own list (Be honest with yourself)
---

2. Embrace New Attitudes Technologies that Really Work

Here are a few new attitudes technologies that I have developed to help me be an effective parent:

It takes more than love to be an effective parent.

Having a child just makes me a leader.

To be a parent I must be responsible for my child until I can teach her to be responsible for herself!

I need to take courses, read books, watch parenting shows, and observe other parents to be an effective parent!

I will expend as much effort raising my child as I put into my income producing job.

Make your own list
---

3. Gain New Information to Create New Attitudes

Personally, if I were President for a day, I would institute a "Parental Licensing Law." That's right, every person in America who chose to bring a child into this world would be required to have a license. No child would be released from the hospital without the "Parental License." Licenses would only be dispensed to parents upon:

☆ **Completion of a "Basic Life Skills Parenting Course"** (teaching how to: bathe the child, hold the child, feed the child, talk to the child, nurture the child, teach the child, love the child, enjoy the child, have fun with the child, etc.).

☆ **A refresher course** would be required for parents of more than one child.

☆ **If parents got a ticket** for any type of child abuse or neglect, they would be required to attend and complete a mandatory "Intensive Remedial Parenting Course." This course would include an "Anger Reduction" segment and a "Positive Parenting" segment before the child was released to their care.

Sadly, I doubt that parental licensing will ever be a reality in America. The next best thing is for us to change our attitudes about parenting.

New information creates new attitudes

You have already started changing your attitudes by reading this book. Yeah YOU!

Now, develop the attitude that you will be the best parent you can be by attending your own private university for parenting. you will graduate at the end of your life on earth. Since it is a lifelong process, you might as well enjoy the ride. Your course work includes:

☆ **Reading parenting books.** Give yourself a deadline or you will never get to it. Decide to read a book a week, a month or a year. Just start!

☆ **Enrolling in parenting courses.** If you cannot find one, and that is a real possibility—we take dog training more seriously than we do raising our children (sorry just a little commentary)—start your own. Ask four friends or neighbors to get together once a month to discuss parenting attitudes and skills. Each couple, or person, is asked to read something about parenting and share the ideas with the group. Include a problem solving segment. Choose parents with different age children so you have a diverse group and can share what you did with your little ones or what to expect from your teens.

☆ **Sharing ideas** on the Internet

☆ **Doing whatever it takes** to graduate as parent of a successful SUPER STAR child!

Parenting is a lifetime learning commitment. Your attitudes drive your behaviors. Get rid of the antiquated attitudes that do not work anymore and replace them with ones that do. Attend your own parenting university. Graduate with honors!!!

Insights and Notes

Attitude Technologies
CHANGE YOUR ATTITUDES AND YOU CAN CHANGE YOUR LIFE

1. You do not have a "Parenting Chip." Develop the attitude that parenting is your most important life's job.

2. Spaced repetition is how you learned most of your parenting attitudes (see it, hear it, or experience it 6 times a day for 21 days— you own it).

3. Rid yourself of attitudes that do not work and replace them with ones that do.

4. Change your attitudes and your behaviors will follow.

5. How do you change?
   Become uncomfortable with your parenting attitudes and skills.
   Embrace new attitudes technologies that will lead you to new behaviors.
   Gain new information and attend your own private parenting university.

4

 Your Most
Important Job on
Planet Earth Is To
Be the Best Parent
You Can Be

In my opinion, two things are needed to raise SUPER STAR (*Healthy, Happy, Self-Assured, Bright, Kind-Hearted, Loving, "Bonker's Free"*) children:

☆ PLENTY OF LOVE
   and a willingness to take the time and effort to learn
☆ EFFECTIVE PARENTING ATTITUDES AND SKILLS!

In all my years of teaching, I never once had parents tell me that they wanted their children to become failures and have miserable lives. Even my most challenging parents loved their children, in their own unusual way, and wanted them to succeed.

> *Most parents, unless they are psychotic,*
> *love their children and want them*
> *to thrive and to be successful.*

Since you are reading this book, I'll assume you love your child, or children, and want them to thrive and be successful. Then why are so many parents stressed out and over-the-edge? What is causing most of the problems in parenting? Lack of a Strategic Family Plan and lack of Positive Parenting Attitudes and Skills.

In my counseling practice, I often saw parents who loved their children. Most of the problems arose from a lack of *positive parenting skills* not a lack of love. When questioned, my clients related they were frustrated because they never saw good parenting techniques by their own parents. Or some said they had watched TV shows like "Father Knows Best" and "The Ozzie and Harriet Show," which were fantasies of parenting in the '50s and '60s, and were frustrated because their children didn't turn out like Ricky and David. Or they watched "Rosanne," who constantly seemed to be baffled or haphazard in her ability to parent her children.

RELIEF...parenting skills can be learned!

Being a parent takes work. Most of the parents I know never gave parenting a thought. They decided to have children and—WHA-LA—little Susie or Johnny was born. They assumed they would be effective parents just because they loved kids. They paid more attention to picking out the room decorations and cribs then they did to planning to be the BEST PARENTS THEY COULD BE!

Can you imagine doing that with your job, vacation, or finances? Not even!!! Each time I changed careers or entered a new field, I did the research.

I needed to know:

☆ How much time and effort would it take to enter this new field?

☆ Would I have to go back to college?

☆ How much would it cost and which school would be the best?

☆ What kind of income could I expect for this new career?

☆ Would I be able to advance in my field, or would I remain in a horizontal holding pattern?

I didn't just wish and hope that my boss would let me keep my job just because I WANTED IT! I had to plan to move ahead in my job and learn the new skills to stay abreast of all the changes or risk a pink slip.

When I vacation I usually find out:

☆ How much it will cost?

☆ How long will I be able to stay?

☆ Does the hotel have non-smoking accommodations?

I don't just wish and hope that the hotel will let me stay an extra week just because I WANT TO! I plan to stay the extra week or risk "NO ROOM IN THE INN."

With my finances I need to know:

☆ Will the bank charge me service fees?

☆ Should I use a financial planner or learn to invest my-self?

☆ What return should I expect on my investment?

I don't just wish and hope that money will appear in my bank account because I WANT IT TO! I plan by saving for retirement or risk having to live on social security. That is a scary thought!

Did you stop and ask these questions before you became a parent? Did you say, "What do I need to know about parenting?"

☆ How much time and effort would it take to enter this new field of parenting?

☆ Would I have to go back to college? Which school would be the best for a parenting degree?

☆ How much would it cost?

☆ What kind of results could I expect for this new parenting career?

☆ Would I be able to advance in my parent field, or would I remain in a horizontal holding pattern?

Be honest, did you really ask these questions of yourself? Or did you do what most families do—just add a child, or children, to your existing life, and then become frustrated because there was never enough time, money or sleep?

We plan our careers, our vacations and our investments . . . IT IS TIME TO TAKE RESPONSIBILITY TO PLAN TO BE THE BEST PARENTS WE CAN BE!

Notice, I said to be the BEST PARENTS WE CAN BE. You don't become an effective parent just because you WANT TO! You become an effective parent, when you PLAN to be the BEST PARENT YOU CAN BE.

That means you are continually learning new skills by reading, taking parenting courses, doing self-discovery exercises, and observing others who possess positive skills. It's the same process you would take if you wanted to advance in your career field. You constantly learn new ideas or you are left behind. Parenting is no different.

When I was an elementary school teacher, I loved children and therefore just assumed I would be a great teacher. Boy, was I in for a big shock! Just because I loved children did not mean I had the skills to manage a classroom. Little things eluded me: how to make the sound of long "A," how to get the students to submit their homework on time, or how to grade papers. Frustration with the little things in the classroom caused frustration with the very students I loved.

*In most professions, including parenting,
prolonged frustration turns to anger and
blaming, and the love turns to hate.*

My problem, as a beginning school teacher, was not lack of love, but a lack of teaching skills. To remedy the situation, I took a day off from school, without pay, to go observe another teacher I thought was particularly skilled. I began to read classroom management books. I went to every seminar and lecture I could find. I stopped trying to be a good teacher or a perfect teacher—which does not exist anyway—and started being an effective teacher. My mission was to become the BEST TEACHER I COULD BE by continually learning new and more effective skills.

The same principle applies to being a parent. Strive to be the BEST PARENT YOU CAN BE! Just because you love your child, or children, does not mean you will have the skills to deal with all their needs. Stop trying to be a "Good Parent." When you strive to be a "Good Parent" you are headed for misery. There will be days you are not a "Good Parent." Your self-talk will kick in, *A Good Parent would not have done that. I must be a Bad Parent.*

Even career criminals, on death row, do not want to be "Bad Parents." Once you are a "Bad Parent" you feel guilty and usually repeat the same behavior at a later date. Being a "Bad Parent" implies that you are inherently bad; therefore . . . *That's just the way I am . . . You can't teach an old dog new tricks . . . There's no way out . . . I'm just not good at this parenting thing.*

Wouldn't it make more sense to strive to be the BEST PARENT YOU CAN BE. Then when you mess up—and we all mess up as parents—you can say one of the following:

Gosh, that was a misguided way to react to the situation, I need to learn to be more patient.

How could I have better distracted my child?

Yelling is very ineffective behavior on my part. The kids have learned to block me out and I feel so awful afterwards. I need to learn another technique to use in this situation.

I didn't mean to lose my temper. I need to calm down before I say another word.

You, and only you, decide when you will start being the best parent you can be. Give up the old attitudes that allow you to stay the same. Learn new Attitude Technologies that will allow you to be the Best Parent You Can Be by being an Effective Parent.

Effective parents give themselves permission to make mistakes and learn from those mistakes. Effective parents thrive with each new challenge and learn new ways to solve challenges. Effective parents strive to be the best they can be by learning new skills and attitudes.

Attitude Technologies

CHOOSE TO BE THE BEST PARENT YOU CAN BE!

1. Stop trying to be a GOOD PARENT.
2. Start being an EFFECTIVE PARENT.
3. Read, study, observe, and learn new attitudes and skills.

   BE THE BEST PARENT YOU CAN BE!

Insights and Notes

5

 Create A Strategic Plan for Your Family

To be the best parent you can be, you must have a plan. Too many families just evolve, with no direction. They steer off course and have no emergency plan to get back on course. Yet, most corporations have a strategic plan. That plan usually includes:

☆ **A Vision**—a clear set of directions or goals to steer the company on a success path

☆ **Corporate Culture**—values of the company

☆ **Training**—for managers , staff and front-line employees

☆ **Individual Action Plans**—for each division to get to the common goal or vision

☆ **Emergency Plan**—when the going gets tough

Most strategic plans start by looking at the history of the company. Reviewing the history helps determine the values that guided the company through the good times and the bad times. Once you know the values of the founders, you can write the vision.

The same applies for your family. By reviewing your family history you can determine your values. Once you have the values listed on paper, you can then choose which values you would like to keep, which values might not be useful anymore and which new values you would like to include in your family history. Once you have chosen the values for your family, you can write a family vision.

Start with Your Family History

Family History is important! Whether you came from a great home or a horrid home, you need to look at your past. It is hard to know where you are going if you do not know from where you came.

I intently listened to the history of my family. The stories of how my parents and grandparents met, how they were raised, and what they valued gave me great insights into why I behave the way I do. My family history gave me information about what I need to appreciate about myself and my family and what I need to change about myself.

> ### Exercise: Write Your Family History
>
> *Write down your family history so that you can take a look at your roots to determine the values with which you were raised.*

For some of you this "Family History Exercise" will be extremely pleasurable, as it was for me. For some of you this will be painful. As a psychologist, most of my clients found this to be a difficult exercise. Until they took a look at where they came from, their roots, they continued to repeat the same mistakes of their family. Until they, literally, saw the family secrets, mistakes, and poor parenting skills on paper, they continued to fantasize that their miserable childhood had happened to someone else. They also believed it was just the way things were. "That is how I was raised so that is how I raised my kid." **It doesn't have to be that way!**

Take the time to discover and know your family history. Examine the positive parenting skills you experienced—whether it came from your own parents, other family members, friends, or teachers—and choose to repeat these patterns. Also examine the negative parenting skills, or lack of parenting skills, and choose NOT TO REPEAT THESE PATTERNS.

When you see your history on paper you can *choose* to keep all the positive attitudes and behaviors. YOU CAN CHANGE even though you might have been poorly parented. You must know what did not work before you can change and substitute what will work.

DECIDE TO BE THE BEST PARENT YOU CAN BE NOW!

Insights and Notes

My Roots

6

Paul L. Mulvaney, my father, came from a farming family in Jackson, Michigan. His parents were hard working, industrious people trying to eke out a living on their farm. Being cautious people they surveyed their "baby farm" and decided it could support two more mouths. After having two daughters, Agnes and Ethel, they decided to take a break and concentrate on building the farm. They waited 13 years before trying again, this time hoping for a son.

Exercise: Write Your Family History

Discover the values your family held, the positive or effective parenting skills your family possessed, and the parenting skills that needed improvement.

Make this exercise fit your personality and family. Write it to make sense to you! Since I'm the author, I wrote it in prose. You might find it easier to outline, use key words and phrases, use picture words—do it your way! This is for you!

When little Paul arrived, his two older sisters were over-joyed at the prospect of having a baby of their own. Dolls had always been considered a frivolous expense, but when Paul was born the two sisters had their very own little real doll. Living with two older sisters who doted on him and treated him like a living doll, Paul received tons of kindly petting and adoration. Although they bossed him around, they also taught him to be self-assured and independent, but Paul was all boy and needed a release. He because the consummate tease, using practical jokes to get a smile from his stoic parents and make his sisters stream with tears of laughter.

Paul was a quiet little boy who loved to read and learn new and wonderful things. Although he was needed on the farm, he was sent to a Catholic school miles away. His aunt was a nun and insisted the family send him to a Catholic school in hopes he would become a priest. Paul had to walk a good distance daily but it never bothered him as he so loved the books and all the new and wonderful things he learned there with the Jesuit brothers. He was so starved for new knowledge that he stole away each evening to silently read the only material he had at home—his dictionary.

Life on the farm was often harsh as Mother Nature was always in charge. All family members were expected to contribute to making the farm thrive and little Paul was not exempt. Each day, after his long journey to school, he was expected to do his part. Therefore, Paul had little time for singing, laughing and being a kid. The emphasis was on surviving and making a living.

Although they weren't overt with their affections, his parents loved Paul. Their mission was to make things grow and survive, and they had little time left over for fun. Paul got most of his praise from the Jesuit priests and his adoring sisters for doing well in school. Since he loved to learn and was exceptionally bright, lots of praise was lavished upon him.

Paul L. Mulvaney
Young man
starting out

As Paul grew, his books took him all around the world. He developed a wanderlust to see, smell, and hear all the things he had read about, but he could see no way off the farm except to become one of the Jesuit brothers he had so admired while growing up. They were always so gentle, kind and accepting.

Paul took the high school classes that would aim him in the direction of serving God through the priesthood. Then one of his teachers discovered the brilliance of Paul's mind, the wanderlust in Paul's heart, and the gentleness in his soul, and encouraged Paul to become a much needed medical surgeon instead. This was exactly what Paul had dreamt about. With the encouragement of the priest, Paul went to his parents to explain his dream of becoming a surgeon and asked for the money to attend college.

His folks, people of few words, denied his request, stating they needed his help. The year was 1936 and the country was in the midst of a depression. Paul had been instrumental in selling all the farms fruits and vegetables in the Detroit market each weekend and the family counted on his help. Secretly, they couldn't bear to let their only son leave the nest at only 16.

Crushed but not dissuaded, Paul knew he would never be able to earn enough to make his dreams come true on the farm and he could see he had outgrown Jackson, Michigan. Against his parent's wishes, he bought a motorcycle and headed for California, where a distant cousin lived. He hoped to get a job in California to pay for college in the big city. Paul soon ran out of money so he sold the bike and began to ride the rails with the thousands of other hobos who were searching for a new life and way to make a living. Paul saw abject poverty, but found he had a curious way of helping each one he met with his gentle ways and easy-going smile.

The world was heating up as Hitler and his Axis buddies began to race across Europe and the Pacific. Paul's patriotic juices were being whipped up by all the advertisements and he was boiling over with desire to join the Navy. When he went down to the station to join the Navy, he discovered he could make all his dreams come true—see the world and become the surgeon he dreamt about. They would train him. There was just one little problem . . . Paul was too young to join on his own and he was the only son in his family. Paul so desperately knew the Navy needed him and he needed the Navy, that he forged his parent's name on the papers to enter the Navy. His guilt overwhelmed him, and he wrote saying that would be the last dishonest thing he would ever do.

Paul loved the Navy! He applied for medical school immediately, but discovered he was too young for the program. However, the Navy saw his obvious talent and said they would train him as a medic until he was old enough to apply for medical school. Paul was elated at being able to learn new things in the field he loved. He soon was sent to Chelsea Naval Hospital in Chelsea, Massachusetts where his life would change again.

Mary Patricia Landry and her girlfriend, Linda Kelly, had gone to Chelsea Naval Hospital to visit a friend. Linda saw Corpsman Mulvaney and waved hello. Paul waved back at Linda but was thunder-struck by her girlfriend. With just one look, Paul knew this was no earthly creature—his prayers had been answered. Paul had been sent this joyous earth angel. He knew immediately he would marry her as soon as he could meet her and find out her name.

He ran out of his office and begged Linda to introduce him to her friend. "Paul this is my friend Mary Pat but everyone calls her Marie." Paul, not wanting to appear forward, made a date with Linda and said he would bring another fellow for her friend Marie. It was decided they would all go out Tuesday night. Then the girls rushed off so they would not miss the bus home.

Tuesday came and went, and Paul and his friend were "no shows." Mary Patricia and Linda assumed Paul was not interested and more likely was just another sailor with too many girls.

Fate would have it that Marie had to go to Chelsea Naval Hospital the next week. Paul dashed out of his office to talk to Marie but she was less than excited to see him and not the least interested. She told him she was not accustomed to being stood up! Paul responded, "I could not find a date for your friend."

"But *you* were supposed to be going out with my friend," Marie said.

Then Paul said, "I didn't show because *you* are the girl I want to date." Paul explained that he never intended to go out with her friend but had full intentions of going out with her. He seemed like such a gentle guy, Marie agreed to meet him and a friend at Revere Beach to enjoy the rides and boardwalk.

As promised, Paul brought a friend for her girlfriend and both couples enjoyed the evening. Marie was so easy to talk

Paul meets the love of his life, Mary Patricia—Marie!

to and filled with such enthusiasm for life that Paul couldn't help himself. He paraded her into a jewelry store and said, "Pick out a ring, I'm going to marry you." Marie, thinking Paul was a big tease trying to impress her and her friends, picked out the most expensive ring, in the case, and everyone had a big laugh. What Marie did not know was the next day Paul returned to the store to purchase the ring. Since he had little money, he began to sell his blood to make the extra cash he would need to ask his Marie to marry him.

Soon thereafter, Paul arrived at the Landry residence to ask Marie's father, David Landry and her mother, Madge McCormick Landry, for Marie's hand in marriage. Marie's father said yes immediately, but her mother was horrified and tried every way she could to dissuade Paul. She sat Paul down to tell him Marie's life story.

She began in her Canadian-Irish brogue:

We are totally different from you and you must know a family before you marry into it. I was born and raised in Newfoundland Canada as an Irish Catholic. We were a large loving Catholic family that loved Newfoundland, but when times got hard, there was no work. At age 26, I was sent to Boston, as our relatives before me had come and written about the riches to be had in America. Although I only got to "Tom's Dog," the 3rd grade reader in school, I was bright and could catch on fast.

As with all immigrants, I went to the Canadian part of Boston to a boarding house that our relatives, who had come before, recommended. There I met David Landry, another French Catholic immigrant from Nova Scotia, Canada. He was so dapper and shy, each night after dinner he would cloister himself away in his room writing letters home to his mother. I was so full of life and mischief that the other boarders began to dare me to get David to talk. Well, I took the dare. One night after David was retired to his room, I stood on a chair and squirted water, through the transom over the door, into his room. Needless to say, this got his attention. He stormed out demanding to know who had ruined his beautiful letter to his mother. I stepped forward and told him I had done it and that I didn't mean to spoil his letter to his mother. I just wanted to get his attention so he would come out and talk, play cards, and have a little bit of fun. Well, don't you know, that did the trick and shortly thereafter we were married.

David was a chef on the whaling ships, and later on the rich people's yachts, and went to sea for weeks at a time. When he came home he wanted peace, quiet, and the love of his growing family. Although I was 29 when we wed, we had eight wonderful children together. Dave asked me to please be in charge of running the home and disciplining the children. He never wanted me to use a threat such as: "WAIT UNTIL YOUR FATHER GETS HOME." When Dave came home, it was time for joyous celebration as he would bring lobster, which to the fishermen, were the scum of the ocean but to our growing family and me it was a delicacy. Even though the house was raucous most of the time, Dave always wanted his children dressed and polite for dinner. The table was always set as if the Queen herself would arrive any minute. Dave doted on the children and delighted in nicknaming each child for their personality traits—your Marie was "Sweet Spirit of Niter." The house was always filled with laughter, warmth, and mischief.

Family is such an important value to us. Dave and I both cared for our aging parents and all the children would help. Of course, we came from rather large families, which we helped to bring over to this country one member at a time. We all settled near each other. What we would do is invite everyone to the house when Dave came home from sea, roll back the rugs, and sing and dance till the wee hours of the morning. Of course, on occasion, we would pass the screech—Newfoundland Whiskey, the libation of the Newfoundlanders, along with the hat for donations to get the next person over. There were always more donations according to the amount of screech that had been consumed. I guess the end justifies the means.

Now to be sure, there was not a lot of money to go around, so I had to be clever with Dave at sea so much. I remember one time, *we needed a new house to rent because of our growing tribe. I knew the landlord would take one look at a Mrs. with eight children, and he wouldn't even be talkin' to me. So, I sent all the children to play in the nearby church graveyard. When the landlord asked, "Do you have any children" I could respond with a clear conscience, "They are all up in the graveyard!" Well, of course, he thought I meant they were all deceased. So thinkin" I was a poor woman who had lost her children, don't you know, he rented me the house. I want you to know I said many a Hail Mary for that little bit of a white lie. Me conscience got the better of me, so right after, I told him the truth. He got such a laugh out of me being so clever that he said he would have rented to me anyway because he had never seen such a helpful well-behaved group of children. The landlord became a dear friend of the family and, Oh! how we would laugh at him renting to a lady thinking she had no children and in reality having eight. You see I always had a bit of the blarney in me.*

To help Dave supplement our income, I would take in renters and do nursing around the neighborhood. Of course, I didn't have the fine medical training that you have Paul, but a lot of those old country remedies worked pretty darn well. Which brings me to telling you about your Marie.

When Marie was born, her sister Katherine—Kay—as we call her, was almost a year and a half old. By the time Marie was one, I was already carrying Tom. With Dave at sea and Marie just a wee one, the local priest thought I should become a foster mother for one of the orphan children. Back then, they brought children to the church so people would adopt them. Gladys was a homely crossed-eyed child and no one would take her. Gladys tugged on my sleeve and said "No one will take me because I'm so homely. Please, can I come home with you. I'll help you with your own children." Well that touched my heart and I couldn't leave her there alone. Dave came home to find we had three children instead of two.

Your little Marie was a glorious child. Happy, happy, happy— she rarely cried and was very active, moving, talking, and walking very early. One night, Dave and I had gone to a wake. We left Gladys, who was about 13, in charge of the children as Kay was almost three by then, Marie was 18 months, and Tom had just been born. When we came home, what a fright we got when we went in to check on the children. Little Marie just lay lifeless in her crib. I knew in just one look, but I said nothing to Dave. I grabbed Marie out of the crib, covered her with the blanket clutching her to my heart and ran all the way to Dr. Strong's hospital, which was in his home, across the street from us. Well, my dear, the doctor took one look and confirmed my worst fear. Marie had infantile paralysis, which we later called polio.

Of course, not a lot was known about the disease back then. The doctors snatched little Marie from me, immediately scrubbed us down and placed us in white gowns and masks. They told us, "Go home! There is nothing you can do!" as they placed my poor tiny limp baby girl in a monstrous looking object called the "iron lung." It was all so terrifying. Although I felt so helpless on the physical plane, the doctors were wrong about us being able to do nothing. Dave and I got down on our knees and prayed to our merciful God, "Please God, help our little Marie and let us have the strength and courage to accept your will."

They transferred Marie to Children's Hospital, so daily I took the MTA to see our little sweetheart. Since, they did not know exactly how the disease was transferred and thought we might be in danger from our own child, we always had to scrub and dress in the gowns and masks. How scared our Marie must have been to see these huge masked creatures leaning over her, but she was ever so brave and never cried or showed her fear. How proud Dave and I were of little Marie because we went home every night and secretly cried as we prayed silently for a miracle.

The days turned into weeks, the weeks turned into years, and Marie went in and out of the hospital, never once whining or complaining. She had such a "sweet sunshiny" disposition that all the nurses and doctors loved her. This gave me the peace to leave her in their care because, sadly, Dave and I could only visit Marie every other week, as our family continued to grow.

When Marie showed boredom with the endless hours of lying in bed with her leg sometimes elevated over her head attached to heavy weights, I would tell her to look out the window: Watch the men mowing the lawns, smell the fresh grass, listen to the radio, learn all the words to the songs, and use her imagination to create fabulous places to visit one day.

As you can imagine, with the doctor bills mounting and the family growing, there was not much money for toys to bring Marie, but we did the best we could. I would bring a jar of olives, which she could eat or, more often than not, Marie would just have to share her treat with the other bedridden children. She invented the "throw the olive game," as she would toss olives to all the children in the ward so they could all enjoy the treat.

Marie had the end bed, near the glass partition, so all visitors that passed by would see her. Marie always sat up the best she could and waved and blew them kisses. Many would stop back by and send in presents as they couldn't believe a child that sick could be that happy. One day the children begged the doctor to kiss the girl on the ward that he liked best and he chose our little Marie. But when he went to kiss her Marie stopped him. She was so embarrassed because she was sitting on the bedpan. He graciously said, " I'll be back later."

Although the doctors still didn't know the cause of polio, they no longer made us dress in gowns and masks. I was relentless in my search for a cure to Marie's polio. Every new operation or treatment we heard about we asked Marie, "Would you try this new treatment. They are not sure it will help or make you walk, but would you like to give it a try." Once again, Marie accepted each new painful procedure with courage and strength, while Dave and I watched in amazement gaining courage and hope from God's gift to us—this little living angel, our Marie.

In between the 15 operations Marie went through, she was allowed to come home with us for short periods of time. First Marie had to be carried like an infant even though she was six, since her legs still were of no use to her. Of course, we wanted to do everything we could to help Marie, so Dave and I would boil meat bones then place Marie in the hot greasy water and massage her legs. This we were told would help to stimulate the feeling in her

Marie and older sister Catherine—before pretty shoes.

good leg. Dave would then raise her out of the water and wrap her as tightly as he could and hold her for hours as all the Newfoundlanders would gather and sing all the old songs. Oh, how Marie begged to be active with the other children, but Dave would softly tell her stories from the ship he was on and she would contentedly listen.

With Marie's courage and persistence, the doctors kept operating until she could wear heavy braces and move herself with crutches. We were all so very proud of her! At home, we often forgot she did not have two good legs like the other children as she could drag herself around the house with such speed. She pitched in with the chores just like all the other children but Marie longed to go outside and play with the other children.

The cruelest experience I remember was the day she wanted to walk down to my sister's house. I kissed Marie goodbye and marveled as she slowly but steadily walked with her braces and crutches down to my sister's house, inch by inch over the uneven pavement. After I went in the house, Marie experienced the cruelty of the neighborhood childrens' ignorance. The children began to chant unkind names at Marie calling her, "Gimpy, limpy, lame duck." She held her head high and continued to limp past them, as we had prepared her to do, when one the children picked up a stone and threw at poor Marie. Since the pavement was so uneven she couldn't move very rapidly and the other children began to pick up stones and heave them at Marie. Finally, my sister heard the screams of terror and raced out to save Marie from further torment and pain. Although we had taught her the poem: "Sticks and Stones will break your bones, but names will never hurt you," the reality was the physical wounds Marie experienced that day healed quickly but the emotional wounds took much longer.

Now, I was more determined than ever to find a doctor to help Marie walk without any crutches or braces. Our prayers were answered when we were introduced to Dr. Lee. He examined Marie and was amazed and surprised at how wonderfully she had developed in spite of the numerous operations and heavy braces. He immediately fell in love with this joyous little girl who so badly wanted to walk and called her his "Sunshine." He came to us for permission to let him try one more operation. He was sure he could fuse the bones in Marie's foot and ankle so that she would be able to walk unaided by crutches. None of us had the courage to tell our dear daughter that we wanted her to go through yet another painful surgery and recovery period. Dr. Lee said he would ask for Marie's permission.

Dr. Lee walked into the room and sat next to Little Marie who was now 12 years old. He truly understood how painful it must have been for Marie to spend most of her young years locked away in a hospital, operation after operation, recovery after recovery . . . always being told 'This is the last operation you will have to endure." With tears in his eyes, he looked into her trusting little face and gently said, "Marie, I know you have heard this before but I promise you, if you will let me try one more surgery I know this will be your last operation. You will be able to walk without braces and you will be able to wear pretty shoes. This I promise you." Marie, without hesitation, took Dr. Lee's face in her small hands and said, "If you can make me walk, of course, I will let you operate. When do we get started." Dr. Lee broke down and sobbed at the courage this remarkable child displayed.

To help Marie recover from this final surgery in a nurturing environment, Marie's physical therapist told us of a camp in Vermont called the Three C's Camp—Camp for Crippled Children. We hated to give her up, for any more time away from home, but we felt she should have a gentle environment to learn how to walk. We were all so very happy to know she would walk without aids when she returned from camp. Dave and I, reluctantly, let her go.

The camp was tucked away in the green mountains of Vermont, and all the children who went were, or had been, crippled. To strengthen their damaged limbs the children were taught to swim. Can you imagine—Marie is the only child who learned how to swim in our family! She felt so special knowing she now could do something physical that none of the other children could do. They gave her daily physical therapy treatments to strengthen her good leg and increase the mobility of her bad leg. They also sang and treated the children like royalty to overcome some of the emotional damage that had been done by the cruelty of jeering people who didn't know any better.

When Marie returned to us, my heart sang with joy as we watched her take her first steps without braces or crutches! Praise be to God! What a day to celebrate! All our family and our extended family came to watch this miracle. Marie had dreamed of having a pair of regular shoes like all the other children so Dave saved and saved so he would be able to take his daughter out to buy her first real shoes. Unlike the other children, Marie had two different size feet, so Dave had to buy two pairs of shoes, a size 5 and size 6, and then discard two of the shoes. But nothing mattered except the look of sheer excitement as Marie tried on her first "pretty shoes."

Well, my dear, it didn't take long for Marie to learn to walk all over the place. Although her father and I knew when she was tired, as she began to favor the good leg, she would never sit down to save steps. Dave would always say, "Marie, let me save you a few steps,

Marie discovers the poem "Character," and makes it the
foundation on which she will build her life and her family.

*what can I get for you?" Marie, knew her father would do anything
for her.*

*When she reached her teens, having one normal calf and one
withered small calf began to cause problems as so many people
began to ask, "What happened to your leg Marie?" Once again my
heart ached for my Marie. I didn't want Marie to suffer any more
than what she already had suffered so I searched throughout Boston
trying to locate someone who could help us. Finally, a man in the
tannery factory said he could make Marie a fake calf out of a
feathered material, which would be able to go inside her stocking.
From the outside, no one would be able to tell she had one skinny*

leg and one regular leg. It was expensive but I would have sold the house to get Marie what she needed to fit in and feel good about herself. It worked, and as soon as Marie started wearing "her leg" as we called it, people barely even noticed that she limped any more because she had such a lovely sweet personality.

Marie has always loved books and reading. She memorized the poem by Albert Norton Parlin from high school and really has always lived by that poem:

CHARACTER
By Albert N. Praline

I would have all young persons taught to
respect themselves, their citizenship, the
rights of others and all sacred things;
To be healthy, industrious, persevering,
provident, courteous, just, and honest;
Neat in person and in habit, clean in thought
and in speech, modest in manner, cheerful in
spirit and masters of themselves;
Faithful to every trust, loyal to every duty;
Magnanimous in judgment, generous in
service and sympathetic toward the needy
and unfortunate;
For these are the most important things in
life and this is not only the way of wisdom,
happiness and true success but also the way
to make the most of themselves and to be of
greatest service to the world!

She and her sisters have filled this house with suitors and her brothers have managed to chase most of them away. We have all laughed and cried and laughed some more as we celebrated Marie's walking, raised money to bring family members over from

Newfoundland and Nova Scotia, christened babies, and praised the Lord for his many blessings.

Paul, now you know about our family and my Marie. She is not like other girls. She will always need expensive shoes because you will have to buy two pairs to get one. She might need expensive medical treatments throughout her life, and she will always need her family to thrive and survive. Marie was taken from us most of her youth, and now you want to marry her and take her away to live in far off lands. Paul, I like you, but I am not ready to let my daughter go—she is only 18 years old. I want you to wait one year, and if you still feel this way after you return from your tour of duty then I will let you marry my Marie."

Paul had sat silently and listened to Mrs. Landry's story about their family and about Marie. Then he gently began to speak. He told Madge that her family sounded like a wonderful place to grow up, and he related incidents about his own family. For every objection Madge had brought up, Paul had an answer:

I will bring your daughter back to visit your family at least once a year. I will always make sure your daughter has the best shoes money can buy. I am in the medical corps so her medical treatments will never be a problem. And I promise to love and protect your daughter till the day I die. I am a good Catholic and will ensure that we will attend mass every Sunday and raise all our children in the Catholic Church. Mrs. Landry, I respect you and Dave and will do as you ask, but I must beg you to let me marry your daughter now. I know she will not be here when I return, because someone else will win her heart. I am not willing to take that risk. Please Mrs. Landry, I want to marry your daughter before I set sail."

Madge was completely unnerved by this young man who was so sure of himself and so sure of his love for her daughter. She had given him every reason why he should not want to marry her daughter; she had pointed out every obstacle and still she could not dissuade Paul. She knew that it would be worthless to continue. This man truly loved her daughter, and she believed he would be kind and loving, so she finally agreed. Paul and Marie were married shortly thereafter.

From the beginning, their single goal was to have a large family with at least 10 to 12 children. However, soon after they were married, World War II broke out and Paul was sent to the Pacific as a medic. Their separation strengthened their union as they spent endless hours writing detailed letters of the daily happenings to each other. As the war ended, Marie and Paul were reunited for a short time until Paul was, once again, called by his country to serve in the Korean War. At the end of the conflict, Paul and Marie were finally reunited for good.

As the years sped by with no children to bless the union, Marie and Paul became closer and closer and ever more in love with each other. They would spend hours together—reading to each other, playing dominoes or scrabble, or just talking about the day when they would "build a little nest, somewhere out in the west, and let the rest of the world go by." Always present was the longing for children.

After seven childless years, they sought medical help. At first, the doctors were convinced the problem was somehow related to Marie's polio; later, they discovered Marie was filled with fibrous tumors. Marie went through several painful procedures and prayed daily for God and all the angels to hear her plea for a family. Soon thereafter Marie got pregnant. Marie, Paul, and their massive extended family were ecstatic.

As with everything else in Marie's life, having children was not to be easy, but the joy that surrounded her left others astonished that she could be so happy while in so much pain. Unto Marie was born, through Caesarean section, a beautiful baby boy whom they named Paul Wayne Mulvaney. Marie's journey to motherhood had been long and quite painful, but one first glance at her only son made the tears of pain melt into tears of joy, that flowed and flowed and flowed. The doctors and nurses sighed in relief that this "peanut" of a gal had made it through this painful birth.

Immediately, Marie forgot all the pain and concentrated on her little baby angel Wayne. After years of hospitalizations, she had learned to concentrate only on the positive and remember the joy. She had learned to erase the pain as quickly as possible—and that is exactly what she did! Marie and Paul lavished all their love and attention on Wayne, and he ate it up.

Marie began praying for a little girl to join her precious Wayne. Since everyone in the family knew she wanted a redheaded little girl, the advice began to pour in from every relative as to what "Poor Marie" should do to make this come to pass. The advice, as outlandish as if was, was taken very seriously by Marie who desperately would try anything to have more children:

Me dear, if you want to have a girl baby then stand on your head after "doing the deed" so the seed can have a better chance of making its way upstream," to "Me dear, if you want to have a redheaded girl baby, then take this picture of the Johnson baby, hang it at the foot of your bed and pray daily to Saint Ann, the saint of miracles, to bring you a similar child.

Marie had been taught to believe with her heart and soul in all the Irish superstitions so without any resistance she tried every idea the family proposed.

Finally, after two more years of painful surgeries and humiliating procedures, Marie, a brunette, and Paul, a jet-black haired man, were blessed with a little redheaded baby girl. The angels had sent exactly the baby Marie had prayed for. Of course, this child did not come easy. Marie had to have another Caesarean, and the doctors cut her bladder by mistake causing her to become violently ill. Although Marie was too sick to even hold her new baby, she danced with joy in her heart. She knew the angels had danced for her in heaven when they sent this little bundle of joy and light. Marie named her Maureen Gail Mulvaney, not just because it was Irish and lyrical and meant "beloved one, gentle spirit" in Gaelic, but after such a big delivery she wanted the initials to be M.G.M. so she could tell the world . . . this is MY MGM . . . My Big Production. Once again, the tears of joy flowed and flowed and flowed. And once again the doctors and nurses marveled at her ability to withstand the pain and show only joy.

Baby Maureen . . . Little M.G.M. (age 2)

Thinking how lucky she was to have been blessed with two precious treasures, Marie daily thanked God for her fortune. Although Paul and Marie did not stop wanting and trying to have more children, they were not as desperate. So when Marie became pregnant two years later, they were a bit shocked but ever so happy to add another jewel to their family treasure chest.

Once again, it was a difficult birth, but Marie and Paul had another beautiful baby girl. Marie wanted to name the child Candice Barbara Mulvaney so the nickname could be Candy Bar, but Paul finally said, "I think Susan Marie Mulvaney would be much prettier." The tears of joy flowed and flowed and flowed. This time the doctors were upset because someone was going to have to tell Marie and Paul this would be the last child they would have.

The doctors were convinced that Marie was too petite and physically frail to continue having children. Since she had already had three very difficult births, any more children might kill this glorious mother of these three adorable children. The doctors were unwilling to let that happen and besides they had found a large tumor which meant she would have to have a hysterectomy. Knowing Marie's life long dream of having a large family, no one wanted to be the bearer of the news, but she had to be told immediately. Marie was sad to learn that she would never have another child, but felt so blessed to have her three little jewels.

With family complete, Marie and Paul spent all their time and energy doting on their children. They spent hours playing, reading, and talking to their children. Marie had waited so long for her children to arrive that every moment was filled with love and joy. She talked to the babies while she did every little task. "Mom is now going to make you some eggs. First, I take the egg and crack it like this, then I will take a fork and mix it like this . . . ." Or she would make pancakes and flip them all over the kitchen, never caring where they landed just so the children screamed in fits of laughter.

Like Marie's father, Paul was away at sea often, therefore Marie did all the disciplining so when Paul was home he could be the family hero. Marie didn't mind one bit as she adored her beautiful children and spent endless time just talking and laughing with them. Discipline to her meant sitting the children down and telling them, "Mommy can't run after you like other moms, so you must listen to her and stay close," or "Mommy gives you all lots of special time so now it is Mom's time to visit with her friend. You may each take one toy and sit quietly and play while Mom visits." Because the children got so much time to be heard, they listened to mom and obeyed. If Maureen, who was the bold one, decided to try a little departure from family rules a gentle "Ah-Ah-Ah" from Marie was all it took to get her to quiet down.

Marie did as her father had done to her and picked a special attribute of each child and encouraged it. Wayne, who was very bright and good with his hands, was encouraged to make things. Maureen, who was athletic, bold and very outgoing, was encouraged to be MGM—a big production. Wee Susan, who was ever so pretty and shy, was encouraged when she showed promise with numbers and calculations. Marie felt since she was away from her family and they had to move every three years or so to a new location that pets should be part of their life to make up for the family members that were so far away. Although Marie had grown up in the city and was terrified of animals, she allowed her children to have any and every pet they wanted. So the house was always filled with cats, dogs, birds, snakes, chipmunk, and an assortment of other pets.

Each child had a special talent and it was encouraged, but doing things together as a family unit was also encouraged. Entertaining each other was a big part of growing up. Whether Marie missed Paul when he was gone or she just missed all the hustle and bustle of a big family . . . entertainment took on a life of its own. Marie would sit down and say, "Okay, it's show time . . . May I now present the Magnificent Wayne . . . Here's Marvelous MGM . . . or Sensational Susan!

After such an outstanding introduction, each child entertained Marie with various talents . . . singing, dancing, or mostly, just being funny. The object was to see who could make Marie laugh the hardest. Each child tried their best to outdo the other two thus providing tons of laughter daily.

Paul provided the physical rough housing when he was around. You could always hear laughter when he would tackle each child and tickle and tease until all the children would pile on him screaming, "Daddy more, more, more." On snowy days he loved to amaze the children with his "Michigan Stunt Man" driving. He would always say, "Don't tell your mother we did this," then he would find an empty parking lot and slip, slide, and skid around the lot in the car until the children would beg to stop as they were getting dizzy.

Paul and Marie did everything as a team. They had agreed on how to raise their children and the basic rules of the house. They also agreed to support each other and back each other up. Fairness and consistency were paramount. As hard as each child tried, they could not go to Mom to get around Dad and vice versa. The rules gave everyone a secure environment within which to stretch and try new behaviors.

Dinnertime was always full of lively chatter. Both parents encouraged new ideas and participation from all members of the family. Although, the saying: "Children should be seen and not heard" was enforced when company came, it was never part of mealtime. Mother usually opened up a topic and then asked a question: "If you could be an animal, which one would you be?" Or she would recite her favorite poem, "Character:"

Then she would take an aspect of the poem and ask how each child could be more generous in service or courteous. Invariably, we would come up with something that was serious but that ended with a joke so we would see mother laugh and laugh and laugh.

Mother was the *queen of household chore motivation*. She had a talent for making household chores into fun events. *Many hands make light work* was her favorite credo, and she used it often. As we all helped clear the table and wash the dishes she would burst into song and get us all to join in.

CHARACTER
By Albert N. Praline

I would have all young persons taught to
respect themselves, their citizenship, the
rights of others and all sacred things;
To be healthy, industrious, persevering,
provident, courteous, just, and honest;
Neat in person and in habit, clean in thought
and in speech, modest in manner, cheerful in
spirit and masters of themselves;
Faithful to every trust, loyal to every duty;
Magnanimous in judgment, generous in
service and sympathetic toward the needy
and unfortunate;
For these are the most important things in
life and this is not only the way of wisdom,
happiness and true success but also the way
to make the most of themselves and to be of
greatest service to the world!

Her style of motivation was always so subtle that you never knew she was leading you into a new household chore. Mother would say, "When you get to be ten years old, then I'll teach you how to iron, or vacuum, or do the wash, etc." We couldn't wait to get to ten to learn the next task.

When I was in high school some of my friends asked me to go to the local candy store. I replied in an excited voice, "I can't today, it's Tuesday, my day to iron!" They looked at me in complete disbelief and informed me that household chores were not exciting and certainly not fun. I marched right home to tell this to my mother.

She listened intently, then began to roar with laughter. She said, "It was fun while it lasted."

Since my father was a Naval officer we moved often. Once again my mother came to the rescue. Even though there were times she did not want to leave her friends or family, she always made the trips exciting and playful. Once when we had moved from Long Island, New York, to Montgomery, Alabama, we children, were very disappointed, to say the least. It was the middle of the summer and no one in our neighborhood would come near us—we thought because it was so hot outside.

Then one day, the lady across the street, who later became my mother's dear friend, came over to give us some needed advice. She told my mother, "Marie, I don't know how you think you are going to make it here in Montgomery, Alabama, the confederate capital of the world. I am a Protestant from Birmingham and they consider me an outsider. You, on the other hand, are a Catholic, with New York plates on your car, and you speak with a Boston accent that no one can understand—which means you are a Damn Yankee! How do you think you will ever make it here?"

Mother threw back her head and laughed saying,"They just don't know me yet!"

That afternoon, Mom took us to the local malt shop. When, once again, no one would talk to us, Mother made an announcement "I'm having an ice cream sundae party at my house and all of you are invited." They instantly got up and followed my mother to our house. We all became good friends and loved our tour in Montgomery, Alabama.

Family was a big value in our home, and each year we took a trip to Boston to visit our relatives. Since mother came from a family of eight we had over 40 cousins to play with and get to know. We also took trips to Michigan to visit our Mulvaney side. It was wonderful getting to go from Boston, the city where we took rides on the swan boats in the Boston Commons, Christmas shopping in Filenes, subway rides on the MTA, to country life where we would bail hay, eat corn on the cob, and go frog hunting. We adored listening to my grandparents' stories of Newfoundland and of coming to this country, and we learned to love and respect our elders.

My mother so subtly would tell us her values that many a time we would not even know she was doing it. She would drop one of her "pearls of wisdom" into any conversation and then continue to talk. For example, mother decided that the age 25 was a good age to wed. From the time we were babies, she would casually drop into any conversation, mid-sentence, "25 is a good age to get married." Then she would continue to talk without stopping. She did this with everything; for example, "I always knew My MGM would be a Big Production one day," "Family is important," "When you go to college," etc. This technique worked so well that not one of us got married before the age of 25.

How blessed I was to have grown up in such a loving, exciting yet playful home. Both my parents were loving and consistent. They not only loved each other but you could really sense they truly enjoyed each other's company. They worked together as a team and supported and encouraged each other.

Thank you Marie and Paul Mulvaney. You were the Best Parents!

I Discovered from My Family History that My Family Valued:

Family—The Mulvaney family loves each other and we stick together through good and bad. Friends may come and go but family is always there. It's okay to fuss and fight but always make up. No matter what you do, family will stand by you.

Spiritual—Having a belief in God is paramount. Being thankful is important.

> Exercise:
>
> *What did you discover from your family history?*
>
> *What did your family value?*

Education—Education is the key to the future. Love learning.

Independence—Because mother was sickly, she wanted each of us to learn how to take care of ourselves, in case, God forbid, something should happen to her. Therefore, she found fun ways to teach us household chores so we could be self-sufficient.

Happiness and Joy—Singing, dancing, and laughing were always part of our daily life. Entertaining, story telling, and being funny was definitely encouraged.

Friends and Loyalty—Navy life meant moving. Every move meant meeting and developing new friendships while holding on to past friendships. My parents continually had friends over to the house and visited friends. My parents were trusting and loyal.

Courage and Perseverance—Although mother had constant pain she never complained or gave up hope. She discovered that joy and happiness lessened her pain, while anger and disappointment

strengthened it. Perseverance was the watch word—
never give up. If you have a dream, follow your
dream. Life can be tough but you just keep on trucking.

Kindness—Kind-heartedness and generosity towards others less fortunate. Mother always had a
cause or a group of people that she helped. We were
encouraged to take the time to help others.

Always Do Your Best—Failure and mistakes are part
of life. As long as you always do your best you will
succeed.

Parenting Skills My Family Possessed

Love—My parents openly displayed loving gestures
towards each other and towards each child. Kissing
and hugging were encouraged by my mother; although it was more difficult for my father, he did it
anyway.

Consistency—If they said it, they did it. If they promised it, they kept their promise. Children become self-
assured when they know they can count on the people
most important in their life . . . their parents.

Fairness—*I don't make cheese of one and chalk of the
other.* As a child I had no idea what that meant. Later
we became aware it meant equal love and treatment
for all. (It is never possible to make everything equal,
because life is not equal, but my parents made a
concerted effort to be fair minded.)

Special Treatment For All—Each child had special
talents and skills. Mother discovered these talents
and positively reinforced them with praise and encouragement. We were each her TREASURES and
each had a special talent.

Teamwork—Parents need to work together with
each other. My parents encouraged one another's

strengths and ignored or reduced the weaknesses. They decided early in their marriage the rules for raising children and agreed to use the same set of rules. They also agreed not to disagree openly in front of the children. If they thought the other parent was mistaken, they discussed it in private and presented a united front.

Discipline—Talk don't spank. Use words to achieve solutions. If adults only use spanking and hitting as a means of discipline, children learn to use only force instead of brains. Think your way out of a problem or use humor to get around the problem.

Parenting Skills My Family Could Have Improved Upon

No matter how wonderful your parents were, there will always be sibling rivalry, jealousy, pettiness, or anger over who got more jelly beans for Easter. After discussing *What parenting skills our parents could have improved upon* with my siblings, none of us could think of one thing my parents could have improved upon. Although we hold extremely different views of most subjects from politics to parenting, we all agreed how lucky we were to have such loving parents. That was a first!

> **Exercise:**
> *Discover parenting skills that needed improvement.*

We did, however, make a list of behaviors that were displayed by one of both parents. REMEMBER: Being aware is the first step to change.

Passive-Aggressive—My father did not openly display anger or displeasure. He would find an annoying way to get back at someone that might have hurt him or angered him. My father used actions instead of words to express his anger.

Super Mom—My mother was super-mom. After having polio, mother believed that being "lame" meant she was "not as good," a second class citizen, because she constantly heard, "Poor Marie, Too bad you have the skinny leg—your good leg is so pretty, Marie has such a nice personality for a lame girl." To compensate for being "Not as Good," mother became better than good. She was SUPER MOM. She did more, worker more and tried harder to ensure we would never be ashamed to have a mom with polio.

OUR FAMILY VISION

My mother and father agreed upon the poem, "Character," to be the vision for our family. Of course, they did not call it a VISION but it was. The poem gave us direction and a sense of what was important.

Mother would say, "The true test of 'Character' is whether you use the ideals of the poem when your father and I are not around." Mother's, non-scientific test, to ensure we were using the ideals of the poem was to watch what we did when we did not think they were around. I'm happy to report, she was usually pleased to hear teachers and friends note our Super Star behaviors.

As I was in the midst of writing this book, my mother called several times and asked, "You are putting

> **Exercise:**
>
> *Discover your family vision.*
>
> *My family did not have anything called a vision back then, but we did have a set of directions to guide our family.*
>
> *Your family probably had a set of unwritten rules everyone lived by.*
>
> *What were your written, or unwritten, rules?*

the poem, "Character," in your book, aren't you? You know your father and I used that to raise you kids. I did tell you that we had eight years before you children came along. That gave us time to observe other people and we put together our plan. Your father and I thought "Character" should be the cornerstone of raising you children." I replied, "Of course, I am putting "Character" in the book! I even wrote the poem several times throughout the book for positive spaced repetition."

CHARACTER
By Albert N. Praline

I would have all young persons taught to respect themselves, their citizenship, the rights of others and all sacred things;
To be healthy, industrious, persevering, provident, courteous, just, and honest;
Neat in person and in habit, clean in thought and in speech, modest in manner, cheerful in spirit and masters of themselves;
Faithful to every trust, loyal to every duty;
Magnanimous in judgment, generous in service and sympathetic toward the needy and unfortunate;
For these are the most important things in life and this is not only the way of wisdom, happiness and true success but also the way to make the most of themselves and to be of greatest service to the world!

Marie and Paul spent 50 wonderful years together!

My Story

SELF-DISCOVERY!
NOW IT'S TIME TO LOOK INSIDE

The next part of developing a Strategic Plan involves looking inside.

This Is My Story

My lifelong dream was to become a mother and a nurse. Being the middle child, I had learned early on how to appease and to please. Since, my father loved education and the medical field and my mom told stories of all the wonderful doctors and nurses who had cared for her, I naturally wanted to be a nurse. Being a nurse would please both parents and it would make me happy as well. Of course,

---

Exercise:

Examine your own story.

Why did you want to have children?

What events have shaped your life——
positively and negatively?

Maureen grows up.

being a doctor seemed more interesting, but girls were encouraged to be nurses instead of doctors, so nurse it was.

My number one mission and passion in life was to be a mother. My own dear mom had been such an inspiration to me and had so loved being a mother; I wanted to be a mom just like her. So, at a very early age I had my life already planned.

After our tour in Alabama, I had particularly liked the southern style of living and chose to go to college at Troy

State University in Troy, Alabama. I was thrilled to be moving toward my dream of being a nurse. After two years in the nursing program, a dynamic and charismatic Ph.D. of Special Education came to our school. She was searching for talented outgoing people to begin her Special Education Program. My name had been given to her as a "go getter" so she solicited me for her program. I was mesmerized and awed by her charm. I transferred right into her Special Education program. Everyone, including myself, was dumbfounded because I was giving up my lifelong dream of becoming a nurse. My parents were disappointed at first but knew I was kind-hearted and great with children so this, too, would be a good field for me, as long as I was happy.

After graduation, I became quite ill. I was sent to my parents' home in Maryland to recuperate. While regaining my strength, I met my future husband. He was an Army officer, Catholic, and came from a family of five whose parents had been together for 40 years. To make sure we were compatible and possessed the same values, we dated for four years. We married, after I turned 25, and began our Army way of life together, which meant we moved every three years.

We traveled the world and loved it. Each new move brought a new job for me. Although I did teach at many of our duty stations, I was not always fortunate enough to find a teaching job. After being stationed in Germany, I went to Boston University to get my Master's Degree in Counseling Psychology to broaden my skill base.

From the onset, we both wanted to have children. After seven years of miscarriages, operations, and disappointments we were still childless. Finally, while stationed in Europe, my medical condition worsened. My physicians felt they were inadequately prepared to deal with my medical challenges and had me flown back to the U.S.A. for surgery. The doctors, my husband, and my parents knew I was in serious trouble yet no one wanted to tell me the truth.

My surgeon, the top man at Walter Reed Hospital, was a kindly older gent. He entered my room and took my hand as he told me the worst news of my life, "Maureen, I know how badly you want to have children but that is not to be. You have massive tumors and the only solution, after the numerous other operations you have had, is a hysterectomy."

I was speechless. This could not be happening. I raced down the hall to the medical library and searched for anything that might give me another option or alternative. Two days later, I showed up in his office and for hours begged him to try one or all of the various alternatives I had discovered. Patiently, he explained why none of these options would work and then brought in several other doctors as second and third opinions. It became apparent, the pain would get worse, my system would continue to break down, and my only viable option was surgery. I would have to have the hysterectomy. I sobbed and sobbed and sobbed!

To make matters worse, my husband was in Europe going through a grueling set of work challenges, my brother Wayne had a herniated disk in his back, and my sister was to be wed that weekend. As always, the family pulled together to get through this tough time.

My family's way of getting through tough times is to laugh. And laugh we did. The Army allowed my husband to be flown in from Europe upon hearing the news of my operation. When my husband arrived, we whisked him off to my sister's wedding to celebrate. The next morning, my brother went in for his back surgery; that afternoon, I went for my surgery—each at different hospitals. By early evening, my brother and I were calling on the phone teasing about who had the bigger scar and who could get up faster. Although the physical pain left me rather quickly, the emotional pain lingered on. For me, this was the death of my real dream . . . to have children. I needed time to mourn but instead I had to immediately return to Europe.

It wasn't the only death I would mourn, as my marriage also began to die. There were many reasons our marriage began to unravel, but the loss of the ability to have children played a major role. After the operation, my husband and I drifted apart. We later divorced. My parents had been married 50 years and his parents had been married 40 years, this seemed impossible to me, yet it happened. I was devastated.

I was on my own for the first time in my life and I did not have a clue what to do. My love of children was so strong; I just couldn't go back into the classroom and see all those little children that I loved so much continue to go home to parents that sometimes did not even seem to care about them. So, I did what I had to do, started all over again in Phoenix, Arizona.

To make ends meet, I began to teach College Psychology and opened a counseling practice. Actually, I made more money teaching second grade than I did as an adjunct instructor, but I loved it. When it became apparent that I would still need to make more money to survive, a friend suggested I try my hand at public speaking. She knew a Texas school system that needed someone to come in and speak for $250.00 and they would pay my air fare to El Paso. I desperately needed the money so I took the job.

Being a teacher for so many years, you'd think I would have realized what was happening. The school system had not used up all their money, so either they brought in a speaker or lost the money for next year. I watched in horror as the superintendent introduced me. "Listen up y'all. We brought this big time speaker in from Phoenix and you are not leaving till you listen to her. We will give you your pay checks at the end of her speech." I looked out on this very macho male angry crowd and thought, "I'm done for."

I knew I needed something to calm this audience down so I reached in my bag and saw a yellow rain slicker. I immediately took a magic marker and put a target in the middle of the back. I walked to the microphone and said, "If my superintendent just told me I would have to sit through some speaker, I would be rather angry. How 'bout y'all?"

"YEAH—you're right about that," yelled the angry mob.

"Well, let's get that anger out. You see that white piece of paper before you. Make it into the biggest, meanest, wettest spit ball you can." They did! Then I donned the yellow rain slicker and turned around. "Take your best shot." They pelted me. Then I said, "Now that you have gotten all that anger out of your system, let's get started." They listened intently for three hours and cheered me on when I finished. I knew that if I were going to have the worst audience of a lifetime as my introduction to the world of public speaking—speaking was going to be my new career because I loved it!

Speaking became my passion and I honed my skills every chance I could, all the while teaching and counseling. When I began making as much in one speaking engagement as I was making in an entire semester of teaching, I quit teaching and focused on my speaking career—which took off like a shot. I was working round the clock but still felt something was missing in my life.

No matter how hard I tried, I could not make the yearning for children go away. Every year that passed the desire for children became greater and greater. I started to review my life. My special education/elementary education background gave me the teaching and parenting skills I would need to be a mother. I earned more than when I had been married with a combined income, and I had a supportive and loving group of family and friends. The answer was simple—I would adopt a child.

Who would have known the path to adoption, as a single parent, would have been so difficult, expensive, and heart wrenching. When you are a biological parent, having a child is simple—you make the decision to conceive and (if you're blessed) you have a baby. As an adoptive SINGLE person, the paperwork and scrutiny is endless. You must meet the state requirements to become a certified adoptive parent, which means you grant permission for a case worker to come to your home and go through your finances, your life history, your home, your family, your friends, and even your backyard. Fortunately, I had a wonderful caseworker who pushed me through the system rapidly; it only took six months instead of a year!

The paperwork is just the beginning. The real work is finding a child to adopt. The least expensive adoption agency in 1990 was $12,000 plus, and it took anywhere from one to three years for placement. In the past, we called that "baby selling" or "baby buying," but today, we just call it adoption.

Because you are desperate to find a child, you go to as many places as possible and tell everyone who will listen that you are looking for a child. You send letters to doctors, lawyers, friends, and family begging anyone who knows a teen or woman "in trouble " to call you because you have a loving home for their baby.

Adoption is like taking a nightmarish roller coast ride through your emotions. Someone calls and says, "My young cousin is pregnant and is only 14. She wants to give her baby up. Would you be interested? " Your emotions soar! You start preparing the room for your new child. Then comes the second call, "Never mind, she is giving the baby to a couple instead," or "We have decided to keep the baby." Three times I was told it was a sure thing, my home was ready to receive my new bundle of joy when three times the mothers changed their minds. This process became extremely costly and emotionally draining. The emotional highs and lows became overwhelming.

After five years of trying to adopt in the U.S.A., I heard about a doctor in Cambodia who was helping divorced, single parents, like myself, adopt orphaned Cambodian children. It was the perfect solution . . . I could save a child from a life of poverty and make my lifelong dream come true.

The challenges and paperwork were astronomical now that immigration services was involved. I had to develop tremendous self-management skills and patience just to deal with the numerous and continuous set-backs.

It became painfully clear that all the money, energy and paperwork would be in vain unless I could fly to Cambodia. Having learned to BE FLEXIBLE while trying to adopt in the United States, I just made the arrangements. I flew to a country with which the U.S. had no diplomatic relationship and flew to Communist Cambodia in the middle of a raging civil war.

I boarded the plane with a friend named Millie Hancock and we made the trek. As I arrived in the well-known "vacation spot," Cambodia, I was ever so excited! I instantly started getting it all on video. I was shooting the scenery when a soldier grabbed the camera and me and threw us up against the wall. Quickly, I negotiated with him; "Please let me keep the camera if I let you keep this money."

I rapidly found out that this was no vacation spot and "gift money"— bribery is such a dirty term—works real well in Cambodia!

When I got to the orphanage, the doctor and agency had selected a six-month-old baby for me. I was thrilled with their selection until I walked through the orphanage door. I instantly fell in love and gave birth through my heart to a gorgeous little one-week-old baby girl. Like magic . . . this little *angel* became soul of my soul and light of my life!!!

Before I had time to revel in the excitement, the next challenge presented itself. If I exchanged babies it would be at least another year to get new paperwork. I began to use all my creativity and communication skills. I asked the orphanage director to switch the babies' paperwork instead. To my surprise, the director said she would do it. Of course, that gift money didn't hurt!

Joyously, I became a MOTHER! I named my angel Mikali—Miki for short—Gie Mulvaney. She would be known as MGM . . . My Big Production!

For weeks we had to stay in scary Cambodia to complete all the necessary paperwork and give out all that "gift money." I just focused on my little MGM. Every minute of every day was filled with ecstasy! Miki was such a gift from above!

Upon leaving Cambodia this ecstasy was quickly shattered. Our paperwork was missing just *one* signature. We couldn't get out of the country. To make matters worst, that same day, I received a fax from my mom. My dear father, who was in the final stages of his battle with cancer, had taken a turn for the worse. The family needed me home. A heartbreaking decision had to be made—stay or go!

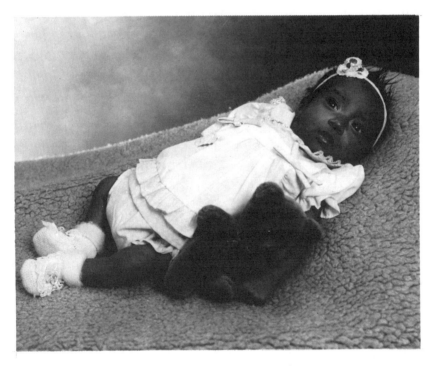

Mikali (Miki) Gie Mulvaney. MGM . . . My Big Production.

Calmly, I focused on the positive. I persuaded two American doctors, who hated paperwork, to bring my baby out if I took care of their babies' immigration paperwork. They agreed! I immediately flew back to the U.S.A. to be with Dad and wait for baby MGM.

It seemed like an eternity, but still focusing on the positive, my baby and I were reunited two weeks later in the United States. Immediately, Miki and I traveled from our home in Arizona to my parents' home in Maryland. My family was overjoyed!

Little Miki was the sunshine, joy and laughter we needed as we watched my dear father deteriorate into the advanced stages of cancer. Everyone, especially my Dad, showered Miki with love. He idealized his new angel grandchild and held her for hours. Miki became his pain medicine.

So, week after week, month after month, our standard routine was to travel from Arizona to Maryland to be with Dad. To keep our spirits up, my mom had the whole house "booby trapped." There were musical toilet paper holders, called, "toitey tunes" in all the bathrooms. The "Star Spangled Banner" played in the main bathroom and, honestly, our guests, who had come to visit with Miki and my dad, didn't know whether to stand and salute or wipe. There were always lots of colorful balloons filled with hot air floating around the house and, trust me, there were also plenty of friends and relatives filled with hot air floating around the house as well.

Oh, how we all laughed. We had already cried buckets of tears for my father and there were very few opportunities for laughter during this time until we were sent a little angel in the form of my Miki. And oh! how Miki would smile and gurgle as everyone held her and showered her with tons of love.

Then, I don't know how to tell you this next part except to say what happened!

The last picture of my father and baby Miki.
(left to right: Marie, Brother Wayne, Dennis, Michael, Carol, John, Maureen, Susan (center) Paul and Miki.

Just four short months later, while Miki and I were at home in Arizona, Miki developed some bumps on her chest. I rushed her to our pediatrician who assured me it was nothing. I told her my dad was in the final stages of cancer and we needed to fly to Maryland. She said, "Go ahead and fly back to Maryland, I'll make the appointment for next week when you return."

When we came back home to Arizona a week later, the unthinkable happened . . . a parent's worst nightmare. My special angel of Joy, Miki, died in her sleep.

Wave after wave of shock was sent though my body as I picked up my lifeless little baby. Just hours before Miki had been smiling and full of life. Now, she was gone and my life was gone too. The police, the fire department, and all my neighbors stormed into the house. They grabbed Miki away from me. At first they said it was SIDS (Sudden Infant Disease Syndrome) but later discovered it was a rare blood disease. It didn't matter, Miki was gone! I screeched like a wounded animal!

Before I could feel the intensity of what had happened, the automatic protective covering of the body—numbness—kicked in! I sat in a daze. I stopped functioning on a conscious level. Oh, my heart beat, my lungs breathed, and my blood flowed but my life was gone. My heart, that had given birth to this child, was broken! I knew I would never be able to Love anyone again like I had loved Miki; the pain of loss was too great!

As this numbness had almost totally encased me and mummified me, the next shock wave hit! MY father, when he heard his beloved little angel Miki had died, let go of life. He died just eight hours after the baby. Half of our family wiped out in one day.

Once again I screeched. How can I describe layers and layers of pain with me sandwiched somewhere in between. There are no words. My heart was simply broken for good.

Eventually, the protective numbness subsided. I'd love to tell you how brave I was but that was not the case. My first response was overwhelming despair. I dropped to my knees and pleaded with God, "Please take me too. I don't want to go on living. My heart is so heavy and my arms are so very empty. Just let me come to you because I can not go on! "

I believe my Higher Power listened to my plea for death. I believe God understood but the answer to me was a resounding, "No, I have a different plan for you." Slowly, without warning, the plan was unraveled for me.

I had sent a letter to all my family and friends exclaiming I had a new little daughter just four months before. Now I had to send a second letter explaining the death of my dear sweet Miki and my father. Upon receiving my letter, a friend named Heidrun, whom Millie had introduced me to in Thailand, called with condolences. Heidrun knew so many people had been touched and helped by my speaking that she wanted to return the favor. She felt my pain and swore she would make it her mission in life to find me another little girl. Heidrun said, "Maureen you just feel better and get stronger, I will begin the search." I answered warily, "Sure, go right ahead," believing this was a kind gesture with no substance behind it.

Several months passed. All of a sudden, I started getting faxes from Heidrun. *I have now contacted Thailand, Korea, and China and they do not allow single parent adoptions.* Boy was I surprised . . . NOT! I was used to disappointment so I really did not even take notice of these faxes until Heidren wrote: *THERE IS HOPE IN VIETNAM!*

While in Vietnam on business, Heidrun had met the man in charge of international adoptions. She told him my story. He was very interested in helping me and he sent pictures of two little girls available for adoption. One child had an eye problem and the second child had a cleft palate. This man, Mr. Nghiem, would be coming to Phoenix of a U.S. tour and would like to meet me.

During our Phoenix visit, Mr. Nghiem said I would be invited to Vietnam and he could clear the way so I could adopt one of the children in the pictures. I was stunned! I had been on this roller coaster before and refused to put out much energy to protect my fragile emotions.

Once again the lengthy and arduous job of immigration paperwork and permissions began. It seemed even more difficult this time because the pain was paramount and the fear was overwhelming. But a little voice kept saying, "This time it will be okay." Could this be THE PLAN!

I flew to Thailand to pick up Heidrun, and together we departed for Ho Chi Minh City (Saigon) Vietnam. When we arrived we were greeted by a contingency from the adoption

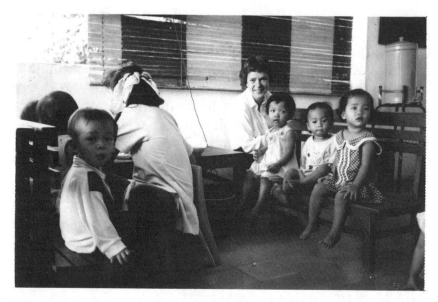

Children at the orphanage in Vietnam—Heidrun is the lady at the back, and she is holding Huong (Mayre).

agency. We were told we would be under the protection of Mr. Nghiem. We were then whisked off to meet little Huong. I gave birth through my heart when I saw her.

There were no written records about little Huong, so the agency director told me what she knew of the child's story: Huong Thi Thang Duong, one and one half years old, was born in a small village in Vietnam. Her parents were poor uneducated peasant farmers. During the birth of Huong, her mother died of acute malaria. Her father was left to care for a very sick baby plus two other small children. Although he cared for little Huong until she was four months old, it became apparent her survival depended on medical treatment. Reluctantly, he took her to an adoption center that provided on site medical treatment, shelter, and caretakers.

The adoption center discovered Huong was malnourished, had a severe cleft palate, respiratory disease, and numerous other medical problems. Most agencies in Vietnam, at this time, were terribly under-funded and this center was no exception. Huong was given medical treatment but her cleft palate went unrepaired. Her constant drooling caused most of her respiratory problems, while repeated ear infections, that went untreated and unnoticed, caused medium to severe hearing losses. The children were given daily food rations, but it wasn't enough and all the children and staff, like the rest of the country, were malnourished. The caretakers were kind and masters of distraction. Each child was touched and individually spoken to as often as possible, but the sheer number of children prevented much individual attention.

Asian culture emphasizes *Be alike . . . do not to stand out*. The center trained the children to do everything as a group: play, potty, eat, and bathe. If a child cried, the caretakers encouraged other children to go over and comfort the child. The caretaker's hand fed every child as quickly as possible, while the other children quietly waited. On even days the children were taken outside for play activities. The play equipment consisted of a Whirl-a-gator, a slide, and one swing. The children did not attempt to venture on to the equipment without a caretaker. The children would patiently wait to be placed on the Whirl-a-gator a caretaker. Once on the equipment, they sat perfectly still waiting for the caretakers to push them instead of pumping themselves. The children seemed to enjoy all the play equipment except the slide. The caretakers would place the child on the slide and every child screamed and cried as they slid down. The only time the children seemed uninhibited was in the confines of their own classroom. They would freely run, shout, and play with each other.

After listening intently to the director, I begged her to allow us to go to Huong's room. Instead, in an effort to make Huong presentable for adoption and save face, the director had Huong dressed in her finest clothes and brought to meet me, by herself. Huong reacted with fear and

*Mommy's little angel,
Mayre, waiting to fly
to her new life and
home in the U.S.A.*

tears. I requested Huong be taken back to her own environment where I would join her.

I entered the classroom and sat quietly on the floor talking with the caretaker holding Huong. Meanwhile, all the other children circled the trio, like little sharks, waiting to see if they could be the chosen one. The caretaker wanted Huong to make a quick decision and said loudly, "Your Mamma!" Huong watched the children begin to touch the lady they called "Mamma" and sensed a decision had to be made quickly. Little Huong wasted no time and leaped into my waiting arms. At that moment, a deep and lasting bond was formed.

We had a few days in Vietnam before we departed. I noticed Huong set herself apart from the other children. She appeared to be embarrassed by her constantly drooling and ashamed that everything she ate, because of the cleft palate, came out her nose. It became my mission to raise her self-esteem and improve her self-image.

The journey back to the United States was very difficult, but both mother and daughter bonded and laughed the whole way back. I wanted Huong to have an instant connection to our family, so I renamed her "Mayre" after her new grandmother. My mother's name is Mary but everyone calls her Marie—Mayre is made-up from MAY and RE. I also wanted to set little Mayre on a success journey so I made Mayre's middle initial G so the initials of Mayre G. Mulvaney would be MGM, a big production. I constantly sought ways to make Mayre feel like a big production to raise her damaged self-esteem.

Everything had changed in Mayre's life and she needed time to adjust. Although the doctors insisted medical treatment had to be immediate, I decided it could wait until Mayre got accustomed to her new home, food, shoes, clothes, and family. Since Mayre did not speak, she showed displeasure or fear by lying on the floor throwing tantrums. I would gently speak to her, touch her lightly, and soon she would stop. To prepare for the numerous operations Mayre faced, we daily dressed in the garb of the operating room, including masks and surgical hats.

One short month later, Mayre was operated on to repair her cleft palate and to improve her hearing. Mayre had no fear of the operating room or staff as she thought it was more play time with mom. After the surgery, Mayre awakened immediately from the anesthesia and started screaming and climbing out of the crib. A nurse raced to find me. The moment Mayre saw Mom she stopped crying and stayed calm while I rocked her. The cleft palate was completely repaired but her hearing was another story.

As I had feared, the operation did not fix the hearing problem. Mayre still had medium hearing loss. Fearing she might lose all hearing, and sensing there might only be a short window of opportunity to teach Mayre sounds and words, I spoke to Mayre continually, describing everything in minute detail. I also made personal phonics rap tapes that we listened to every time we drove anywhere. I intensified her phonics training, sound work, and speech therapy, but also fought to have the doctors try other surgeries to improve the hearing. After a second operation, Mayre had only a mild hearing loss.

My passion became teaching Mayre the love of learning. Having come from a loving environment where my parents made learning a game, I did the same for Mayre, devising games for everything. Mayre was awakened daily with a hug and a song. Music and three-by-five cards, strategically placed on the floor, guided Mayre to each morning activity. A song was created to teach Mayre everything from learning words to brushing teeth to combing hair to learning address and phone numbers. Using music and phonics, Mayre began to read at age three. My natural playful personality lent itself to teaching Mayre everything through music and dance.

Mayre, who had been starved for personal attention, loved all the attention but I sensed she missed being part of a group. I searched for the appropriate preschool with a caring environment for Mayre to continue her love of learning. After two attempts, I located a Montessori school with the perfect environment for Mayre. Daily, I ran Mayre to school in a stroller, all the while, singing and describing everything. I worked closely with the teachers to ensure my values were the values used in class. Mayre was reading at a fourth grade level doing 3-digit math in preschool. The school nurtured both Mayre's creative and analytical sides and she excelled.

Spaced repetition, used extensively in my speeches, was used with Mayre. I told Mayre at least six times a day, every day, YOU ARE A WINNER . . . I LOVE YOU VERY MUCH . . . YOU ARE A SUPER STAR! Mayre's Aunt Susan made a mirror inscribed I AM A WINNER so every time Mayre looked at herself she would read those words. Knowing applause is singly the most powerful motivator of children, I constantly sought opportunities to applaud all Mayre's attempts at reading, eating, and playing. I brought Mayre, at age four, up on stage, in front of 2,000 participants, to bask in the applause of the audience. Mayre thrived on the attention and applause!

I provided Mayre with acrobatic, dance, art and music activities but it became apparent Mayre's forte would be music. Once again I searched for the proper environment in which to place Mayre. Yamaha music school gave group and private lessons. Parents and children were asked to sing, dance and play piano each lesson. The lessons were fun yet highly effective and both Mayre and Mom loved them. Mayre began to play piano and create her own music in a relatively short period. At age eight, Mayre's own composition won a regional competition and Mayre participated in her first out-of-state recital. Even though Mayre was one of the youngest children to participate, her happy-go-lucky manner and self-assured stage presence won her the most applause and favorite performer status. Mayre walked off the stage saying, "Can I start my next composition . . . this time I would like to have a choir sing while I play!" One week after the recital, Mayre asked to play violin and was enrolled in a violin class similar to her piano class. Already she has distinguished herself as a Super Star violinist.

Mayre began her life with little hope of succeeding. Now, there is little doubt she will be anything but successful at everything she attempts. Mayre's success is unlimited!

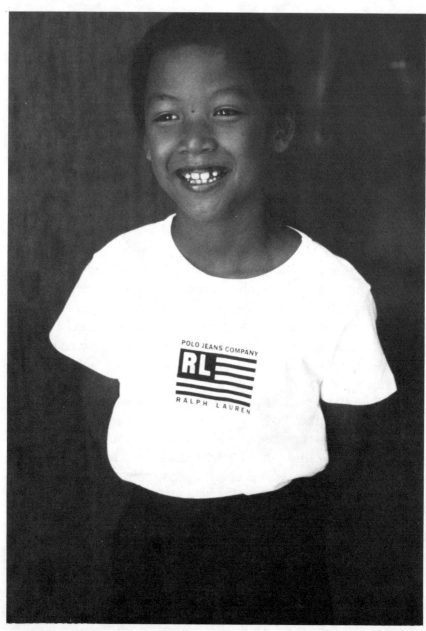

Mayre, the All American Girl.

SELF-DISCOVERY EXERCISE

WHY DID I WANT TO HAVE CHILDREN?

Positive Reasons for Having Children

1. I wanted to be like my mother.
2. I love children and have a child-like personality.
3. I had experienced wonderful parenting skills. I thought I might be able to pass those skills on to my child.
4. I taught for many years and learned many effective teaching skills. I wanted to pass those skills on.
5. I had a parenting plan.

> **Exercise:**
>
> *Why did you want to have children?*
> *Be honest with yourself. State your positive reasons and your less than positive reasons. Honesty can be painful but the results are ever so helpful.*

Less Than Positive Reasons for Having Children

1. My child will be all the things I am not.
2. My child will never leave me.
3. My child will always love me.
4. I'll never be alone.
5. My child will watch over me when I am old and gray.

**Be Aware
Choose to Change!**

I am aware that:

1. I struggled to have children and must guard against smothering my daughter for fear of losing her.
2. I must choose to teach independence over dependence so my daughter will be strong. I am in the helping profession and tend to be a "helper." Dependence would make me feel needed but it would be destructive for my daughter.
3. I must be aware that my daughter is an individual—not my clone. I choose not to live through my daughter but to encourage her talents and individual skills.
4. I must be aware that my daughter will one day grow up and leave my home. I will encourage her to become who she is, not who I want her to be. I will choose to be independent and self-sufficient myself. I will guard against being needy by letting her know I highly desire her company but also have my own life to live. I will let her know she will always be welcome in my home.
5. Continually learn about myself and continually learn new effective parenting skills.
6. I choose to engage in loving relationships with a life-partner, friends and family.

Being aware is the first step to change. If you are not aware you have tendencies to behave in a certain way because of the events in your life, you will never change. But once you see these events on paper, it becomes much clearer what you must do to change.

Taking action is the next step to change. Knowing what needs to be changed is important. Taking the time and effort to change is even more important.

You may choose to read this book and do none of the exercises. You will pick up many good ideas and probably make a few changes. But if you are serious about becoming the Most Effective and Best Parent You Can Be—then write it down. Although, I, like you resisted at first doing some of the exercises, putting your thoughts on paper is magical. Make Some MAGIC!

Be aware of your history.

Take action to keep what was effective and worked.

Discard what was ineffective and did not work.

Write it down. Seeing is believing. Make some magic!

Insights and Notes

Create Your Own Family Vision

So you say, "Create a FAMILY VISION? DUH . . . I don't even know what a *vision* is!"

Well, you are not alone. I was confused between a VISION and an ACTION PLAN until I had my house built. The builder presented me with a blueprint. He said, "This is what your house will look like."

I looked at him blankly and said, "Say what! Your blueprint doesn't make sense to me. I'm not a builder. I do not have an idea of what my house will look like! Could you please draw me a picture or build me a model, then I'll know what my house will look like?"

Vision is the overall picture or model of what you want your family to be.

Action plans are the blueprints or the way you will get to the picture or model. If you know what you would like your family picture or model to look like, then you can devise action plans to get to the picture. MOST FAMILIES DO NOT HAVE A VISION. Without a clear concise Vision, members of your family do not know what is expected and easily go in the wrong direction.

What if I asked you to go to your back yard and shoot some arrows. You would soon become bored just shooting arrows into the air and would begin to look for a target. What if your sister happened by, wouldn't she make the perfect target? (Of course, the arrows have rubber tips and would not hurt her but it sure would annoy her.) Wouldn't it have been a better choice to START WITH A TARGET so you always have something to aim for?

Put up a target . . . YOUR FAMILY Vision . . . members of your family team have something to aim at.

Exercise:
Create Your Family Vision Or Mission Statement

If you are just starting your family, you create the vision, like my parents did. Agree upon your goals and direction.

If you are already an established family, then I suggest you allow all members of your family team to create the vision. Family members will only support what they create. If you create it for them, they will not want to support it.

Once again, make it for your family, your way. Make it a poem, mission statements for each member, talking points—it does not matter the form, just that you take the time to do it.

Speaking of time, taking the time to complete these exercises saves your family hours in the long run. Take the time. Just do it!

OUR VISION

The Mulvaney (Mayre and Mommy) Family Vision

Mom's Mission

To Raise a Healthy, Happy, Self-Assured, Bright, Kind-Hearted, Loving, "Bonker's Free" SUPER-STAR (Mom wrote this).

Mayre's Mission at Eight Years Old

Mayre will have a Fun, Successful, Easy, Enjoyable School Life so she can become a Super-Star Piano Player, Violin Player, and Family Doctor (Mayre wrote this).

We Mulvaneys pledge to each other to:
(Together we wrote this)

☆ Always stick together as a family through the good times and the bad

☆ Believe in God and be thankful for our many blessings

☆ Love each other "second to God" (as Mayre says)

☆ Give back to society by helping people

☆ Value, respect and enjoy each other

☆ Encourage our strengths and improve upon our weaknesses

☆ Love learning and continue for a lifetime

☆ Take responsibility for what we do and what we think

☆ Have a strong sense of love, pride and trust

☆ Have confidence and know we will be successful at what ever we attempt

☆ Learn from mistakes and go ahead and try new things

☆ Know when we mess up we must make up

☆ Accept challenges, take risks, persevere

☆ Attain and maintain excellence (Mom's job is to make the money; Mayre's job is to excel in school, piano and violin . . . while enjoying every minute)

☆ Be honest and tell the truth, even though, you might get in trouble

☆ Recognize and CELEBRATE SUCCESSES as much as possible

☆ Laugh and play and have fun every day.

My original vision was in place before I adopted Mayre. I started from day one teaching her the values of our family. As she grew, I started to include her in the planning. Each year we re-evaluate our plan. We add new items or we subtract items that no longer fit. Each year we both sit down to re-evaluate, sign and commit to abiding by our plan.

The Mulvaneys—Maureen and Mayre—A Big Production!

Hints for Making This A Working Viable Family Vision:

1. Have all family team members participate in making the vision. (Having a vision and plan before your children arrive is ideal. But if you did not have a vision before you had children, you can always develop a vision at any time—even when the children are grown. It's never too late!).

2. Have all family team members *approve* the plan.

3. Have all family team members *sign* the plan.

4. Have all family team members *commit* to the plan.

5. Post the family vision in a prominent spot. Make copies for all family team members, and go over it often, so it becomes part of the family dialogue.

6. Test the vision by observing your children or asking about their behavior when you are not around. Test the vision by observing your parental modeling.

Caution: Notice I said test the vision—I did not say test your children. If your children are not using the vision in daily life, then the vision needs to be changed, or the skills to get your children motivated needs to be changed, or your parental modeling needs to be changed. Model what you value in the vision.

TAKING ACTION

Don't you feel great! You have now created MOST of your Family Strategic Plan:

☆ Family Vision—a clear set of directions or goals for your family.

☆ Family Culture—the values by which everyone will abide.

Now comes the fun part, bringing the family vision— family picture to life. In corporations, once the vision is established they begin to take action. First, they train new staff or retrain mature staff to get to the goal—the vision.

If you are just starting as a family, begin with training. If you are an established family then you will have to re-train. Re-training is much more challenging than training because family team members must change. You can do it if you have a common goal to be the best family you can be!

Start by reading and gathering new information from books, movies, TV, Internet, and other families. Everyone is tasked with coming up with ways to get to the family vision. This is not just a job for parents. Everyone is included.

Once you have gathered the materials, start coming up with new ways to relate to each other.

Part Two

Techniques, Strategies, Games and Recipes to Help Your Child Become A Super Star

The following chapters contain some of the techniques, strategies, games and recipes I used to help Mayre G. Mulvaney become a SUPER STAR.

9

 # Discover Each Child's Special Talents

Mother named me Maureen Gail Mulvaney so the initials would be M.G.M., her Big Production. Throughout my entire life, even now, my mother still uses my initials to encourage me to be a Big Production. As my friend, Patricia Fripp says, "The number one fear in the nation is speaking; number seven is death. That means, more people would rather die than get up and speak." Yet I grew up to be a speaker. Just a coincidence—I don't think so.

My siblings and I were all positively programmed for success by Mom. She recognized the talents each of us had, and started nurturing those talents when we were very young. My mother observed my brother was good with his hands. She continually encouraged and praised him for being so good with his hands. Wayne grew up to be a plumber. Mother observed my sister was good with numbers and details. She continually encouraged and praised her for being such a fine Math Wizard. Susan grew up to work for EPA in Congressional Records, Washington, DC. Mother observed I loved to perform and make people laugh. She continually encouraged and praised me for being so funny and witty. I grew up to be a professional speaker. Just a coincidence—I don't think so.

When I began to write this book, and was having a moment of indecision whether to proceed or forget the whole thing, my sister gave me these words of wisdom. "Of course you should write the book. Mom always called you MGM, a Big Production. You are supposed to do something really big with your life. It is your destiny." Positive programming works.

POSITIVE PROGRAMMING

Discover YOUR CHILD'S Unique Talent

Give your child a variety of options from which to choose. Then sit back and observe.

I was a tom-boy as a child and loved to play all sports. To keep in shape as an adult I ran in the 10K runs. Naturally, when I adopted Mayre, I put her in a baby runner chair, and continued to run. People along the way would comment, "Wow, your little one is going to make a fine runner. She is built like an athlete." Instantly, I jumped ahead 20 years in my mind, and was thrilled at the prospect of developing a Super Star Olympic athlete.

Before I took off with the idea of having a Super Star Olympic athlete in the family, I stopped and observed **what Mayre showed interest in.** It was not sports. She seemed bored with sports, but her face lit up when she heard music.

At age one and one-half, Mayre could barely hear anything. But after all the operations, Mayre began to hear. The first time she heard music, she went wild. She loved it. She immediately began to dance and twirl. From classical to rock and roll, Mayre loved music.

Not wanting to give up on the idea of sports, I began giving Mayre lessons. I wanted to provide her with a variety of lessons so we could discover what her talents were. She took piano, dance, and gymnastics. She thrived and excelled with the piano lessons. She tolerated the dance lessons, but

Super Star Violinist . . . Mayre G. Mulvaney . . . MGM . . . A Big Production!

loved being on stage for the recital. Sad to say, she seemed terrified of the gymnastics, even though the instructor was wonderful. It was a chore to get her to go each week. It did not take a rocket scientist to see Mayre was interested and excited about music, not sports. Music and the performing arts are her fortes. I still encourage other talents so she will be well-rounded, but it would be foolish not to acknowledge her super talents.

Discover Your Child's Talents, Not Yours

Although I wanted Mayre to be an athlete, her talents were in music and the performing arts. I had to set my dreams for her aside and let her be who she was intended to be.

Start Positive Programming by Encouraging that Talent

Mayre is a child who could not even hear when I adopted her, now she is performing before large audiences playing the piano. I know this is a miracle, but I also know the power of positive programming.

Every time Mayre sits down at the piano to play, I introduce her. Although there is no one else in the room, I still say:

> *Ladies and Gentlemen . . . Boys and Girls . . . introducing Mayre G. Mulvaney, MGM . . . Super Star Piano Wizard. Today she will be performing her scales. Then I wildly applaud.*

Applaud and Introduce

The number-one motivator of children is applause. Use it frequently to encourage your children. Use introductions. It worked for P.T. Barnum . . . let it work for your Super Star! Whatever talent your child displays—math, science, reading, singing, sports, art, whatever—applaud and introduce.

Start Sending Your Super Star Mail

All children love mail! Start sending your children mail to encourage them. That's right, actually mail your Super Star child a letter addressed to her. Or if you do not want to spend the 33 cents, place an addressed envelope in with the regular mail and say, "You have a letter." I often will make it a fan letter for Mayre, "Mayre, I am your biggest fan. Keep up the good work!" If you are set up for e-mail, then you can e-mail your child an encouraging letter. Kids love to open the computer and hear, "You've got mail."

My mother sent letters to all of us encouraging our individual talents. Mother encouraged everything from pictures in kindergarten to stage performances as an adult. It only takes three minutes to sit and write, "I always knew my MGM would be a big production one day . . . I loved your picture, or your poem, or your whatever." How excited we were to receive this mail.

Give Your Child A Surprise for Lunch— an Encouraging Note!

One of my favorite ways of encouraging is the lunch box. As I make the lunch each day, I include a *Mom Napkin*. I keep a box of Magic Markers next to the napkins. It takes a nanosecond to write a note. I encourage everything from great piano practice to completing the school homework assignment. Mayre never knows what to expect. It's a surprise each day at lunch time. I used to put notes in the sandwich, but the notes got soggy. Not a great idea but a nice try.

If you are a *Lunchable* kind of parent, just throw a napkin or a 3x5 note card in with the *Lunchable*. If your Super Star eats at school, put a note in his or her backpack. We always select a backpack that has a compartment for *Mom Notes*.

Put your Super Star on a Positive Note Trail!

To encourage Mayre to play the piano, read a book, or do her homework, I will often leave a trail of 3x5 notes. The notes are placed on the floor outside her bedroom in the morning. As she comes out, she sees brightly colored 3x5 cards directing her to the piano to play a piece, to the kitchen to read a poem, or to the bathroom to brush her teeth. Of course the last card always says: YOU ARE A SUPER STAR!

(You can purchase neon colored 3x5 cards. Colored cards are so much more exciting than white ones. It takes a few minutes to write the cards out. I then color code them for reuse at a later date—pink set on Monday, blue on Wednesday, etc.)

101 MESSAGES FOR ENCOURAGING YOUR SUPER STAR
(Messages by Children & Their Parents from Valley Children's Hospital—Fresno, CA.)

You're on the right Track!

That's the Super Star way to do it!

You're doing a great job!

You did a lot of work today!

Who knew you were so good at . . . !

Now you've figured it out

That's RIGHT!   That's the way!

Could you teach me to do that!

Now you have the hang of it.

Did you know your were so talented!

You're really going to town.

You're doing fine!

I can't wait to tell grandma what a great job!

Now you have it!   Nice going!

You look like you enjoy working hard!

That's coming along nicely!

That's great!   Excellent!

You sound like you are enjoying learning!
You did it on time!
Great!   Fantastic!   Terrific!
I think you've got it!
Nothing can stop you now!
Tremendous!
You outdid yourself today!
You're doing beautifully.
How did you do that?
That's better!   Much Better!
You did that all by yourself!
Good job, (name of child).
That's Gold Medal Work!
That's the Best you've ever done!
Good Going!   Keep it Up!
That's over-the-top!
WOW!   What talent!
Couldn't have done it better myself!
That's really nice!
Keep up the good work!
Good for YOU!
I wish I could play piano like you!
Exactly right!   SUPER!
That's the best I've ever heard!
Nice Going!
You make it look so easy!
You make my day!
I've never seen anyone do it better!
You're doing much better today!
You look so happy!
Way to Go!   Awesome!   ENJOY!
Way Cool!   Superb!

You've got that down Pat!
You're getting better everyday!
You've got it made!
You really worked hard today!
I'm so proud of you!
You're very good at that!
Good Remembering!
Marvelous!   Wonderful!
You've got your brain in gear today!
You make my job fun!
That's the way to do it!
That's the best ever!
That's quite an improvement!
I knew you could do it!
You've just about mastered that!
It's a pleasure to teach you!
You must have been practicing!
You haven't missed a thing!
Sensational!
That's better than ever!
Congratulations!
That was first-class work!
You are the greatest!
Right On!
You figured it out fast.
I Love You!
You remembered!
Well, look at you go!
You are special!
You are so good at . . . .
I like that!
You are a winner!

One more time and you'll have it!
You're really learning a lot!
You are loved!
You have been working hard!
You're a Super Star!

Exercise:
FOCUS ON EACH CHILD'S TALENTS

List talents, special aptitudes, and interests
for each of your children.

List ways to encourage your children in these areas.

Create your own list of "Super Star"
messages of encouragement.

Insights and Notes

10

Starting The Day Off in A Super Star Way

The first encounter of a significant nature that you have each day has more impact than the next five encounters as far as your thinking and your attitude are concerned!

One of the fondest memories of my childhood is the gentle loving way my mother awakened us each morning. Her sweet voice would be the first sound of the day. She would gingerly rub our backs as she said, *Wake up my little jewels— sapphire and diamond* (of course, she used this on the two girls; for my brother she would say *my little lump of gold*). *It is time to wake up and start a new and wonderful day.* Then she would sing one of the zillion songs she knew from "Zippitty Do Da" to the "Good Morning School" song.

Mom would allow us a few stretching moments and then we would rise and be ready to start the new day. There was no yelling, "Get out of bed NOW!" Just an instinctive knowledge that those few beginning moments of each day were precious and made the difference between being prepared emotionally to take on the new day or face the day as drudgery.

So you say, "I'm not a morning person. I just can't be perky in the morning." Then fake it until you make it. Can you imagine walking up to your boss and saying, "I'm not a morning person. I will perk up by mid-day, but don't bother me until then." You would be given a pink slip so fast it would make your head spin. Of course you wouldn't do that; yet, it's perfectly alright to do this to your children. CHANGE YOUR ATTITUDE. Model positive behaviors!

Some of you are already whining, "I don't have that kind of time in the morning." Well, it takes just as long to yell, "Get Up Now!" as it does to say "Wake up my little jewels." Which do you think will produce a more positive attitude for the day and a Super-Star start?

BEGINNING AND ENDING THE DAY POSITIVELY

Know that the first experience of the day is the most significant. Make it your mission to start your child's day off with a few kind words.

Often we are more than willing to do this with our preschoolers, but this technique also works with your grown children. By the way, teach your children to do this for you on the weekends. It is wonderful! As you talk or sing to your child, rub her back lightly, take a feather and tickle him, or just hug her or him.

Super-Star Wake Up Ideas

It's time to rise and shine my little Super-Stars.

God has made a new day, open your eyes and greet it.

You are my pride and joy, I'm so glad you are my child.

My life is so much more wonderful since you were born.

You light up my life.

I love you second to God.

(This was created by my loving Mayre)

Good morning my Mayre. Mommy loves you.

My heart is bursting with joy to see your smiling face this
   morning.
Looking at you makes me smile, I can't wait to see the
   rest of the day.
You are one of God's greatest creations.
You are My favorite child in the whole wide world.
If I could choose any child in the world it would be you.
It's time to wake my special
   one.
God blessed me with a child
   like you.
You are Joy and Love rolled
   into one.
Good Morning, Ms. Wings.
You are my morning Angel.

Exercise:

*Make up your own
Super-Star morning
wake-up statements.*

Sing to Your Child Each Morning

You don't have to sing a "real" song, you can make up a special song for each of your children.

Good Morning, Good Morning, the best to you this morning . . . good morning, good morning my Mayre.

Mommy loves her Mayre . . . Mommy loves her girl . . . Mayre's mommy's favorite . . . Best Girl in the World.

Use the old Elvis song . . . Get out of that bed and rattle those pots and pans . . . With a little boogie-beat.

I know what you're thinking. *I just can't sing . . . I couldn't even carry a tune in a bucket.* Okay, then do a RAP, a poem, or just make up a prayer for your child. Perhaps you might even want to repeat the Family Vision day after day. It doesn't have to be long, just special. Let your child know he or she is loved each and every new day in the **Special WAKE UP Way!**

Remember, the first event of the day is the most significant for the entire day. Make rising a SUPER-STAR event.

My mother was way ahead of her time. The poem "Character" was what Mom wanted her family to live by. Daily she read this poem to us. At the time, she didn't know the technique was called SPACED REPETITION, but the results were the same . . . we all knew the poem and lived by it. (Before you go wild thinking it takes soooooo much time . . . read the poem and time yourself. Less than a minute. Surely you have a minute for each child!)

CHARACTER
By Albert N. Praline

I would have all young persons taught to
respect themselves, their citizenship, the
rights of others and all sacred things;
To be healthy, industrious, persevering,
provident, courteous, just, and honest;
Neat in person and in habit, clean in thought
and in speech, modest in manner, cheerful in
spirit and masters of themselves;
Faithful to every trust, loyal to every duty;
Magnanimous in judgment, generous in
service and sympathetic toward the needy
and unfortunate;
For these are the most important things in
life and this is not only the way of wisdom,
happiness and true success but also the way
to make the most of themselves and to be of
greatest service to the world!

Conscientiously Choose Your Expectations

Each morning repeat what you would like your child to
be—for example:

*Mayre, you are a Healthy, Happy, Self-Assured, Bright,
Kind-Hearted, Loving, "Bonker's Free" SUPER STAR!
You are the love and joy of my life.*

Children will live up to your expectations. BUT . . . Be
very careful what you expect!

I once had a student named Tommy. He would arrive at
my classroom each and every day with the weight of the
world on his shoulders. I rarely saw him smile. I was very
concerned and immediately began to think some big trag-

edy had happened in his life of which I was obviously unaware. I needed insight from his parents. I called and left a message to please come in so we could chat.

The next day his mother arrived. As she breezed into the room, she appeared to be extremely irritated with life in general. She came prepared to do battle and started right in, "I don't know why I had to come all the way down here. You are the teacher; you should know what to do with him because, Lord knows, I don't. He just can't seem to do anything right. His father is no help because he is rarely home. Everything is up to me and I just don't know what to do. I try but Tommy just can't do anything right."

In the first five minutes of our visit, I knew why Tommy was the way he was. The mother was extremely frustrated with her life and had few skills to help Tommy with his life. Because her attitude was *Tommy can do nothing right*, Tommy believed he could do nothing right and lived up to her expectations. I had to give the mom a new way to relate to Tommy.

I began to speak, "Mrs. Joy (not her real name, of course) it would be ever so helpful if you could tell me all the things you do like about your son Tommy or all the things that Tommy can do well?"

"Ms. Mulvaney, I just can't think of one thing."

"Mrs. Joy, do you mean to say there is nothing at all that your Tommy does right? Well, does your son Tommy know how to use the bathroom? I mean is he potty trained?"

"Ms. Mulvaney, what a stupid thing to ask . . . of course, he's potty trained. He's in third grade. You should know that!"

"Mrs. Joy, does Tommy have friends? Do kids ever knock on your door and ask if Tommy can come out and play?"

"Ms. Mulvaney, of course Tommy has friends. They are always running in and out of the house."

"Mrs. Joy, does Tommy know his ABCs? Can he read?"

"Ms. Mulvaney, of course he can read. He is in your third grade, you know he can read!"

"Mrs. Joy, can your son Tommy run, jump and play?"

"Ms. Mulvaney, of course Tommy can play . . . that is all he ever wants to do!"

"Mrs. Joy, does your son Tommy ever have any chores that he is supposed to do?"

"Ms. Mulvaney, of course Tommy has chores. He has to make his bed every day, pick up his clothes, and clear the table."

"Mrs. Joy, does your son Tommy ever say I LOVE YOU?"

"Ms. Mulvaney, of course Tommy says he loves me."

"Mrs. Joy, this is my last question. Is your son Tommy ever well behaved."

Mrs. Joy began to smugly grin, "Ms. Mulvaney, I got you on that one! The only time my Tommy is ever well behaved is when he is sleeping!!!"

I hesitated a moment, then I asked, "Mrs. Joy, do you love your son Tommy?"

"Ms. Mulvaney, of course I love my son Tommy! I love him very much."

"Mrs. Joy, would you like to help your son Tommy?"

"Ms. Mulvaney, if I knew what to do to help Tommy, I would do it."

"Mrs. Joy, I have a plan that will greatly help your son Tommy. **You must be committed to doing what I ask you to do for 30 days without stop.** You must do exactly what I ask you to do or it will not work."

"Ms. Mulvaney, I'll try but I need to know what the plan is first."

"Mrs. Joy, I want you to stand at the door of your son's bedroom every night before you go to bed. I want you to watch him as he sleeps peacefully. Then I want you to list all the things you love about your son and all the things Tommy does right. I do not want you to TRY to do this, I want a commitment that you WILL do this!"

"But Ms. Mulvaney, maybe you did not hear me in the beginning—I've already told you that Tommy does not do anything right!"

"Oh Mrs. Joy, I did hear you. You have already told me all the things that Tommy does right."

"Are you daft? I never told you anything that Tommy does right."

"Oh, contra, Mrs. Joy. You told me:

Your son Tommy can use the bathroom . . . therefore, your son Tommy is Potty Trained.

Your son Tommy has friends . . . therefore, your son Tommy is Friendly.

Your son Tommy knows his ABCs, he can read . . . therefore, your son Tommy is Bright.

Your son Tommy can run, jump and play . . . therefore, your son Tommy is Athletic.

Your son Tommy can and does do chores . . . therefore, your son Tommy is Responsible.

Your son Tommy says I LOVE YOU . . . therefore, your son Tommy is LOVABLE!

And lastly, you told me that your son Tommy is only well behaved when he is asleep . . . therefore, your son Tommy SLEEPS WELL BEHAVED."

Mrs. Joy, I want you to stand at your son's room every night for 30 days and every morning for 30 days and whisper:

I love my son Tommy because he is potty trained.

I love my son Tommy because he is friendly.

I love my son Tommy because he is bright.

I love my son Tommy because he is athletic.

I love my son Tommy because he is lovable.

I love my son Tommy because he sleeps well behaved!

Mrs. Joy thought I was completely absurd. But before she left my classroom that day, I extracted a promise that for 30 days she would religiously stand at Tommy's door, the first thing in the morning and the last thing at night, and say I LOVE YOU BECAUSE . . . I assured her this would take less than three minutes per day. I then scheduled a follow-up session with her at the end of the 30 days.

At the end of the 30 days, Mrs. Joy showed up at my classroom with a smile on her face. She told me Tommy was a different kid. She said, "I did exactly what you told me to do. Every night and every morning I stood at his door and whispered all those things you wrote down for me to say."

"Well, Mrs. Joy, it must have worked if you think Tommy is a different kid."

"Oh, Ms. Mulvaney, I don't think it was anything I did, it must be all that extra attention you are giving him here in class. Thank you for all your help."

Before Mrs. Joy left I extracted a promise that she would continue to stand at Tommy's door and whisper attributes she would like him to have. When she balked and said she didn't think it would work, I just smiled and said, "Well then, do it just for grins and to humor me." She promised.

Be the Change Agent

Mrs. Joy did not realize that she was the *Change Agent*, not me. As long as Mrs. Joy thought Tommy could do nothing right, she had to find examples of Tommy's poor behavior to be right. When she changed her attitude toward, and perception of, Tommy, she then began to seek examples of things Tommy did correctly so she could be right. Then Tommy had to live up to all the new perceptions Mom had. Instead of a vicious cycle, this becomes a POSITIVE PERCEPTION CYCLE. By changing her attitude about her son, he changed his attitude. Tommy began to live up to his mom's new expectations.

Make your list of attributes

Take the time to sit down and write out all the attributes you like about your child and the things he or she does well. Parents of teens often complain, "Are you crazy! there is nothing about my teen that is okay right now." If you are letting your teen drive you crazy and are so frustrated that you cannot think of anything positive, then wait until the teen goes to bed. When you are sure your teen is sound asleep, stand at the door of his room and watch him! See him peacefully sleeping. Remember a time when he was a joy to be around. Then make your list of attributes. After you've listed all the positive attributes, make your list of attributes you would like your child to develop.

Children will live up to your expectations. Make sure you **consciously** know what you want for your children. Then repeat it daily to yourself and whisper it to your SUPER STAR. When you believe, your child will believe.

Exercise:

List all the attributes you like about your child and all the things he or she does well.

List all the attributes you would like your child to have.

Insights and Notes

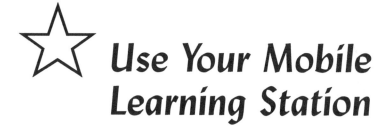

Use Your Mobile Learning Station

In an age when everyone is doing more with less, or should I say doing less with less, time has become a more precious commodity. No one today seems to have enough of it. Therefore, we must conserve as much as possible and use each and every situation as a valuable learning opportunity. Remember what your kindergarten teacher used to say: USE YOUR TIME WISELY!

To me, there is no more valuable time then "Drive Time." It is time to turn that automobile into a **MOBILE LEARNING STATION**. Think about it—there really isn't a better time to learn or a more suitable setting within which to learn—you have your child's complete undivided attention (no TV, no friends ringing the doorbell asking "Can Mayre can come out to play?" no reports that you are concentrating on, etc.). This is a marvelous opportunity to turn wasted "traffic wait time" into fabulous "**CHILD AND PARENT FOCUS TIME.**"

The first year of preschool, I ran Mayre to school each day. While running, (okay, I mostly huffed and puffed and walked fast), I would point out every tree, shrub, bird, bus, school . . . she was just learning words back then. I would sing songs to her and make up songs to teach her words and sentences. But when I changed her school, distance and time constraints prevented our run time. It became more convenient to drive Mayre to school. I immediately missed our learning and bonding time. Then it dawned on me . . . I could turn the car into a learning station so we could continue our bonding and learning.

CREATING THE MOBILE LEARNING STATION

1. GET EXCITED THAT YOU HAVE FOUND A SEGMENT OF TIME TO TEACH YOUR CHILD SOMETHING NEW AND WONDERFUL!

2. Turn the radio OFF. The radio is a distraction that you can do without for the precious time you have with your child.

3. Make sure you always have a basket of books in the back seat for your child. This gives your child something to look at and handle during the times when you have to get off automatic pilot and really concentrate on the road and other traffic. If you choose, learning games and learning toys are okay, but please leave the GI Joes and Barbie Dolls at home.

4. Make a big deal out of entering the "MOBILE LEARNING STATION." My dialogue with Mayre would go something like:

   We are now entering the MOBILE LEARNING STATION. Make sure you fasten your seat belt and engage your brain. A whole lot of learning is about to go on. The count down to learning is about to begin. 10...9...8...7...6...5...4...3...2...1...Blast off into learning!"

5. Start collecting learning cassettes (you might want to create one of your own). Our favorite tape was the one I made that had the alphabet, sounds, and words on it. Because the doctors feared Mayre would lose

her hearing, I was on a mission to teach her to read as early as possible. This way, God forbid, if she should lose her hearing at least she would be able to read. Daily, our drive time was truly learning time. If we arrived at our destination before the tape was over, we often would sit in the parking lot listening to make sure we got the whole session in. By listening to the alphabet and sounds every day for a year, needless to say Mayre had a tremendous foundation in phonics. It was a mere, hop, skip, and a jump to combine the sounds into words. I am convinced this daily repetition set Mayre on a reading adventure that hasn't stopped. She was reading on a fifth grade level by the time she was only five years old.

6. **Begin the MOBILE LEARNING STATION as early as possible.** If you did not start this when your child was an infant, don't worry, start now. You can listen to classical music, books on tape, critical thinking, or motivational tapes. (Call 800-485-0065 or e-mail mgmul@aol.com for the MGM motivational tapes!) Kids, even the big ones, really do love to learn. Make learning fun and exciting and they will also love to learn. Model that you are interested in learning. Use your auto as a *Mobile Learning Station.*

Insights and Notes

12

 # Avoid Being A Giant Parent Slot Machine

Have you ever taken your normally well-behaved adorable child for a public outing, only to be horrified by outrageous, demon-like crying and wailing when you refused to purchase some item your child wanted? You watch in a stunned silence as your child proceeds to embarrass and frustrate you in front of family, friends, and strangers standing in line behind you. Of course, your instant reaction is to stop this little alien creature from further torturing you, but you don't want to be taken away in handcuffs as a child abuser, so you just stand there frozen as your child terrorizes you.

CHILD "CHECK-OUT TERRORISM"

Child: "Mommie, may I get Spiderman?" or "Mommie, I want Spiderman!"

Mother: "Honey, not today." **First NO**

Child: "Mommie please let me get Spiderman, I don't have this one."

Mother: "Baby, no you can not have that today."
Second NO

Child: "I want Spiderman . . . Tommy has one and I want one!"

Mother: "I said no." **Third NO**

Child: Begins to cry as you near the check out stand, "You never let me have anything, we never have any fun."

Mother: "Now honey, I said NO." **Fourth NO**

Child: Escalates pleads . . . intensifies crying . . . lots more tears, "But I want Spiderman! Please get him for me."

Mother: Feeling embarrassed and guilty for her child's behavior says, "All right, get Spiderman but just stop that whining," then whispers in the "I Mean It" voice, "You just wait until we get to that car."

Why does this "Check-Out Terrorism" scenario continue to happen again and again and again? Because **parents are like giant slot machines to children—even to the big ones**. Your child pulls "your handle" with pleads, cries, and whines. You resist with No, No, No, until your patience level is worn down and your embarrassment level is up. Then your child goes in for "the kill" and tries just one more time . . . BINGO . . . it took your child four pulls on your "NO handle" until he or she got to the pay off—the toy!

The parent is held hostage by the child's inappropriate behavior at the precise moment the parent is the most vulnerable and filled with embarrassment and guilt . . . Check-Out time! Check-out time games works so well because there is always a long line behind you and, of course, you know what the other people in the line are thinking: *Hurry up and get that whiny child out of here, you are holding up the whole line.*

The minute you gave in and bought the item for your child, you taught your child a very valuable lesson:

I, THE PARENT, WILL BE YOUR GIANT SLOT MA-CHINE! It might take you 3 to 10 to 15 NOs, but if you

whine at the right time and in the right place . . .
BINGO . . . I will pay off EVERY time and you will get
the toy, the attention, the drink of water at bedtime, etc.

Your child, genius that she or he is, has discovered WHY GAMBLING WORKS SO WELL! You see, the Las Vegas slot machines work the same way as we "Giant Parent Slot Machines" work. YOUR CHILD ALREADY KNOWS THE SECRET!

PARENTS, PAY ATTENTION!
Here Is The Secret: Intermittent Reinforcement

Slot machines work so successfully because they use what is called intermittent reinforcement—you never know when the pay off is coming! The gambler never knows when there will be a pay off, so he or she continues to pump tons of coins into the slot machine while pulling the handle in hopes there will be a Big Pay Off. Often times in Vegas you will even see grown adults putting on a show, either yelling or screaming at the machine or saying, "Come to momma!"

If the slot machine paid off every time, you would eventually get bored and stop playing, even though you were making money. If there were NO pay offs, you would get frustrated and stop putting money in. But, most slot machines pay off INTERMITTENTLY, which means you never know when it is going to spit out coins! Therefore, you willingly put coin after coin in the machine, pull the handle time after time, while yelling encouragements at a machine . . . 3 to 10 to 15 times until . . . Bingo . . . PAY OFF!

Gosh, is it any wonder that your child pulls on your "No Handle" . . . 3 to 10 to 15 times . . . while whining, crying, sniveling, yelling and screaming in anxious anticipation of the PAY OFF. Your child waits patiently, puts on a show for everyone, and finally gets you to pay off.

Stop Being A Giant Parent Slot Machine!

When Mayre was two and one-half years old, I used to take her to our local K-Mart almost daily for our entertainment. (Okay, okay . . . so we live in Phoenix . . . trust me, there is just not a lot to keep you entertained when the temperatures soar to 120 degrees.) Seeing an opportunity to kill two birds with one stone, I approached our Local K-Mart management with what I thought was an exceptional idea.

Dear K-Mart Management:

As a parent, I would spend more time in your store shopping if you would kindly provide a few kid vehicles and/or kid shopping carts so my child would be entertained as I shop. The children could ride around the store and deposit the vehicles at the door on the way out. This would keep the children entertained, parents would spend more time and money in your store, and it would provide a valuable learning experience for the children so they would shop K-Mart in the future!

Well, don't you know, our local K-Mart loved the idea! They provided carts and Lil Tikes cars for the children to ride around the store while parents shopped. I thought this was very entertaining and would help teach Mayre valuable lessons:

☆ **Responsibility**—Please don't run into other people and stay on your side of the aisle.

☆ **Sharing**—Since Mayre is an only child, I wanted her to learn that all toys do not automatically belong to her. Some toys are for everyone to share.

Every day I would tell her, "Mayre, K-Mart ONLY allows kids to borrow toys. Children always must leave the toys in the store for others to share. We don't take toys home with us. (I thought that was very clever because every time I bought a toy that Mayre loved in the store, she never touched it at home. By telling her at age two that we didn't take the toys home, I thought this would put an end to the "I-want-it syndrome.") So daily, Mayre played with the toys in the toy aisle and dropped off the kid's shopping cart at the check-out counter with no tears, pleads, or power struggles.

Then one day she watched another child scream for a toy as the mother went through the check-out counter. The child ended up getting the toy. Being a vicarious learner, the very next day, Mayre got to the check-out counter and started to cry . . . "Mommie I want a toy." I gently told her we always leave the toys at the store to share with the other kids. For the first time she wasn't buying my strategy and escalated her crying and pleading.

NOW . . . this is when you must be a patient parent. You have to make a decision: Do I stop now and take care of this behavior, even though it will take some time, or am I in a big hurry and think I can deal with it later? There is no choice: Deal with it the first time, or deal with it every time.

So, I consciously made my decision. I told the check-out lady I was sorry but my child was telling me with her crying behavior that she did not want to purchase any items. I said we would be back the next day for our items. I gently picked Mayre up and walked out of the store. I stood quietly just outside the store without a word to Mayre while she really cried. When she slowed down to take a breath, I said,

> **Deal with it the first time, or you will deal with it every time you shop!**

Mayre, you are a wonderful child and Mommie loves you very much. You chose not to show appropriate behavior in the store so Mommie brought you out here. I think maybe you forgot the rules for appropriate behavior, so let me help you. I will buy you items when you ask appropriately, but Mommie is not like other moms . . . I will never buy you a toy when you are whining and crying. I love you enough not to let your inappropriate behavior work to get what you want. Mayre, don't worry, I will always give you another chance to practice appropriate behavior. We will try again tomorrow."

We walked to the car and went home.

STOPPING THE "CHECK-OUT COUNTER" TERROR

1. Don't Let Your Child Hold You Hostage

Decide not to be held hostage by your child at check-out time or any other time while at home or in public. Realize that no matter how wonderful your child is, Check-Out Terrorism is something most kids will try at one time or another. The key to eliminating this inappropriate behavior is to **BE PREPARED.**

2. Action Plan for Check-out Terrorism!

Have your plan of action ready at all times so you don't "Just React" to the situation and your momentary embarrassment in public. (Remember . . . if you forget your plan and react by just buying your child the whined for item . . . don't despair . . . you can try again the next day.)

☆ First, please know, whining, crying, and begging for a toy is not some grand scheme designed by your child to drive you crazy . . . it is just **intermittent reinforcement.** If your child has ever whined or cried and gotten the desired store item or toy from another sibling. . . or drink at bedtime . . . or whatever . . . your child is HOOKED on you being a Giant Slot Machine. Your child will continue to "play you" (whine, cry, and plead) while waiting for the pay off (the toy, drink, attention from you, etc.) until you, the parent, PULL THE PLUG!

☆ Daily, let your child know you expect appropriate behavior at all times whether you are out in public or at home.

☆ Set your rules in a fun and easy to learn manner. Then your child will enjoy learning plus remember the rules.

☆ Go over your rules for appropriate behavior as many times as you can within a short period of time.

Rules for Appropriate Behavior

Mayre, I want you to know Mommie loves you and wants you to be the best you can be. Let's go over the rules for appropriate behavior one more time!
Mommie is always happy to listen to any request when:
you ask politely with a please,
you look up at Mom and ask in a clear pleasant voice,
you say thank you.
If Mom can honor your request, I will politely tell you yes; but if Mom cannot honor your request, I will give you information to let you know why I cannot honor your request.
No whining or sniveling by either Mayre or Mom.

Consequences for Inappropriate Behavior

Mayre, if you forget and start to whine and cry when we are in public, Mommie will stop everything, kindly tell the store clerk we must leave, and I will take you outside. If we are at home, mom will ask you to go to time out.

Always Give Your Child Another
Opportunity to Learn Appropriate Behavior

Parents, when you depart the store, you do not yell or scream. You stand quietly and wait for your child to calm down. When your child stops long enough to take a breath, quietly say:

You told me by your behavior that you did not want to remain in the store. Remember the rules:
Mommie will always listen to any request when you ask politely with a pleasant voice and say thank you. I guess you forgot all the rules when you started to cry and whine. That is okay, we all forget sometimes. I am willing to give you another try but not until tomorrow. Right now we must go home so we can practice the appropriate behavior game.

Parents, Always Give Yourself Another Opportunity to Learn Appropriate Behavior

If by chance your child catches you in an off moment and you react instead of using your action game plan, forgive yourself and start over as soon as possible. Let your child know you are sorry for your inappropriate behavior and that you will use better judgment the next time. Model the behavior you want. If you mess up you must say you are sorry and make-up!

3. Practice, Practice, Practice!

Once your child has been given the rules of appropriate behavior, it is time to practice. I liked to have a couple of dry runs with Mayre before going to the store but if you start at the store, be sure you are willing to leave your items at the check-out stand if need be.

Let Your Child Practice the Appropriate Behavior Game

Ask your child:

Do you want to pretend to be the parent or the child?

Let your child choose the role. Then say,

If you are the parent, then you must teach me, the child, the rules of appropriate behavior and show me what will happen if I forget and use inappropriate behavior.

Role play with your child several times until he or she knows the rules and sees how much more pleasant it is to be around well-behaved people.

4. Don't Resist!

Before you say you don't have the time . . . understand that EACH time you give in to your child's sniveling, whining, and crying you give your child permission to do it again and again and again. You also give your child permission to treat you as the Giant Slot Machine. Pull the Plug!

5. Try this Technique at Least Seven Times

As I have said previously in this book . . . SPACED REPETITION WORKS. Remember, you must not give up. If your child does not stop whining on your first attempt, try at least seven more times, consistently.

Set certain expectations for purchasing items for your child at the store. When children are young, expect that they will behave and ask for items in an appropriate manner and take care of those items after purchase. For older children, ask that they decide what item they want and save up for that item, work at home for that item, or creatively get other siblings to help purchase that item for everyone.

> *Don't buy your child, or children, everything they want the minute they want it.*

Although we want our children to have our same value system, we continually give our children different values by just handing them "everything." We say: "Work hard because I want you to be responsible" yet we turn right around and give our children everything they want with no expectations or consequences.

Insights and Notes

13

Take A Lesson from Theme Parks

Mayre once attended a preschool class at a near-by nationally owned day care center. After one week, I noticed Mayre's behavior rapidly changing. She was saying words I had never used at home and barking out orders. I asked where she learned this and she said at school. Although I had observed the teacher, I went back to observe unannounced. I saw the teacher constantly yelling and barking out orders. I went to the director, and told her this was unacceptable behavior. I volunteered to help the teacher learn new skills to stop the yelling. The director did not accept my offer and the teacher continued to yell. I immediately took Mayre out of the center.

If you want respect you must model respect. Yelling, demanding, and ordering children around is not a respectful way to talk to children. You, as an adult, would never put up with that kind of treatment. Can you imagine one of your co-workers saying to you, "I said pick up those reports right now!" or "Do it because I SAID TO!" or "Don't you give me any of your lip!" You would be appalled and probably quit!

Actually, this style of ordering and barking out orders came directly from the U.S. Army. During WWII, officers barked out orders so soldiers would respond without question in battle situations. In a battle, hospital emergency, or any kind or emergency situation, the ordering communication style is acceptable. But it is not acceptable to talk to anyone, child or adult, in an ordering, barking manner during peace time.

You might have heard this style of communication as a child. Therefore, you mistakenly thought it was acceptable to talk to children in this manner. After all, you are the adult. Please, do not speak to your SUPER STAR in this manner. If you have gotten into the bad habit of ordering, demanding, and barking out orders at your children . . . STOP immediately. This type behavior does not work.

Instead, do what they do at theme parks! Have you ever taken your children to a theme park and observed how they get the children to do just about anything they want?

At Epcot center in Florida, you should see how the Disney Cast Members (people who work at the park) get very high energy kids to sit quietly and do exactly what they want them to do. How do they do it?

LEARN FROM THE DISNEY CAST MEMBERS

Disney renamed their Theme Park Staff . . . Cast Members, which indicates that everyone has a part to play in the Magic Kingdom. Each part is valued and honored. Everyone is needed and each task is considered important. Although there are certain Cast Members in charge of trash, each Cast Member is encouraged to pick up trash whenever they see it.

Most successful corporations today have formed teams, because studies have indicated this is a more enjoyable and much more productive way to work. When people form communities, or teams, and participate together, there is greater connectiveness. People take responsibility and become more productive. Everyone feels needed and every task is considered important.

Rename Your Family

Make everyone part of the Family Team. Call them Family Team Members, Cast Members, VIP Members, whatever makes sense to you. Allow team members to come up with their own name.

☆ **Define the tasks within your Magic Kingdom.** Once again choose your own Family Theme Park name. (Our family theme park is called "Mulvaney's Irish Acres; our family team members are called "Leprechauns!)

☆ **Pick Your Favorite Task.** Ask each team member to choose the tasks they want to be responsible for each week. The tasks that no one wants to do are put on a rotating basis. Every team member is encouraged to take responsibility for his or her area. Everyone is encouraged to help out other team members when they get behind. Everyone is encouraged to help out with the trash.

☆ **Hold weekly encouragement sessions.** These meetings serve to remind Team Members that everyone is needed to make the Family Magic Kingdom run efficiently. If one member does not take care of his task, others must pick up the slack. As a family community everyone is expected to help out! Do not, I repeat, do not make these sessions into NAG sessions. If a task is not being completed, ask:

> *Is there is a problem? How can we, the family team, assist you in completing this task next week? I want you to know you are a valued team member. We need your help to make our family run smoothly.*

☆ **Teach the task in a fun manner.** The Disney Cast Members used various techniques to get the children ready to watch a performance.

> *It's great to have you here today. We have some rules I would like you to follow, will you help me out . . . Yes, yelled all the children!*

When I touch my nose—Laugh

When I touch my chin—Go WHOOOOOO

When I count to 3—Make Noise from any part of your body

Teach your children house rules in this same FUN manner

☆ **Pretend to put on walking shoes** . . . have your children pretend to put on their walking shoes also. Then say, "Now that you have your walking shoes on, there will be no running—only walking in our house."

☆ **Ask your children**, "Why do Minnie and Mickey have such big ears?"
TO HEAR—That's right.
And now everyone put your hands straight up in the air, now make two fists and bring them down to your head. Now, you too have Mickey and Minnie ears. Whenever I raise my hands to my head like this it means I want you to listen very carefully with no talking. Now let's try it.

Teach your children household chores in this same FUN manner

My mother had us doing all sorts of household chores. We thought they were fun because Mom would sing, dance, and carry on with each task. "Whistle while you work," was a favorite. It was in high school that we were informed by other friends that household chores were drudgery. It doesn't have to be that way!

> *Your child deserves the opportunity to learn independence and home skills. Make it Fun!*

Household chores teach confidence, responsibility and self-assuredness. Of course, you don't ask a three year old to carry a plate of spaghetti across to the dining room table, but you can teach a three year old to carry a napkin. Make it fun and make it age appropriate. Set your children up for success to be Super Stars! It takes many small successes to make a Super Star.

Children want to help when they are young. LET THEM! Teach your older children, who might have missed this fun part of life, the joy of helping now! LET THEM HELP!

☆ **Build on small successes to create larger successes.** (As always, if you did not teach the tasks when they were young, start where they are now!) My plan was to teach Mayre small chores and move to the larger chores.

☆ **Set the stage for excitement.** We Irish love story telling. Tell the stories of your childhood or of members of your family. If you did not have a particularly enjoyable childhood, then tell the stories you have heard from other people or books. Make these stories relate to the issue at hand. If you want your child to do household chores, then tell the stories of the chores you had to do. If you want to teach a virtue like honesty, then relate those kinds of stories.

☆ **Tell the task they will learn next and at what age.** "Mayre, when you make it to age five, I will teach you how to set the table for our Magic Kingdom. I learned to set the table at age five. Of course, you will have to know left, right, and all the silverware names. We can start learning some of these things before age five."

Mayre would be so excited to get to the next task she would often say, "Please Mom, I think I am ready now."

To keep the excitement going, I would reply, "Well, I don't know Mayre, age five is when I learned to set the table, but maybe you are just a bit more prepared then I was, okay, okay . . . I'll give you a test run.

I would let her put the place mats, napkins and silverware in place. She would have to put the silverware in its correct spot on the right or left so it helped her learn left and right. Then the next week, I would allow Mayre to carry the plates to the table. Step by step, she learned to set the table. Each new step gave her a feeling of pride and accomplishment.

For all of you parents who are balking, "My child can't learn household chores." Delete that attitude right now! I have watched little five year olds walk into the video arcade, select a machine, put the money in, and begin to play. Personally, I can't even figure out where to put the money. Then I hear the parents of those same children say, "I would never think about letting my son or daughter do the laundry." Honey, if they are old enough to play video machines, they are old enough to play the laundry machine. Give your child the opportunity to play your very own video machine at home—the dishwasher or the washing machine.

Your child deserves the opportunity to learn independence and home skills. Don't take those opportunities away—they have so few nowadays. When I was a child, I jumped on my bike the moment I got home from school and raced to the park to play "Red Rover" with all the other neighborhood kids. I learned to go down the street by myself, get back home by myself, and to freely spend time with other children.

Today, our children don't have that freedom. We cannot allow our children to walk even three doors down without monitoring them because we live in a very different society. If we do not give kids opportunities to test skills and make mistakes, they will never learn to be independent and confident. Give your Super Star household (Magic Kingdom) chores as Cast Members in your family.

Mayre makes her first Communion. Yeah . . . Mayre.

Insights and Notes

14

☆ **Celebrations**

As a part of our Family Vision, we celebrate just about anything and everything. We celebrate all the normal holidays: St. Patrick's Day, Easter, Christmas, New Years, birthdays and anniversaries, but we also celebrate everything in between. The mere suggestion of a celebration sends a clear message that this is IMPORTANT because we are celebrating it. Therefore, whatever your family values . . . celebrate!

Education is important to our family. We always celebrate the first day of each school year, a new reading book, science projects, advancement to the next math concept . . . if I want Mayre to be excited, I celebrate.

Celebration does not mean you go out, rent a hall, and invite all the relatives and friends, although for big occasions we do. Celebration, to me, means make it seem important by putting emphasis on it.

Mayre went to the Ahwatukee Foothills Montessori School for Preschool and Kindergarten. All students were given a beautiful aqua blue bookbag when they completed all their phonics and were ready to start reading. Every child was desperate to get to that bookbag. Why?

☆ No child got the bookbag unless he or she did the work.
☆ There was a sense of pride that the child had completed the work necessary to advance to reading in real books.

☆ Each child was celebrated in class for getting to the BOOKBAG!

A small celebration, actually just an announcement, meant a big deal because they did it themselves. The announcement celebrated their accomplishment. When Mayre got her BOOKBAG, I made a big deal of this. We celebrated! I had a small cake made at Dairy Queen which read YOU CAN READ! . . . GREAT JOB . . . MAYRE! I then invited our neighbors over for a 15-minute celebration. My neighbors walked in, said "good job," had a piece of cake, and out the door. Time is a precious commodity, but so is your child. He or she is SURELY worth 15 minutes!

Celebrations do not have to be elaborate or take a lot of time. You just have to remember to celebrate.

HINTS FOR CELEBRATING

1. Be Selective What You Celebrate

Celebrate what your family values. In the beginning, when you are trying to motivate your children to value learning, math, piano, violin, spiritual events, sports, etc., celebrate often. As they get older, taper off and only celebrate larger accomplishments. For example:

> *In preschool I celebrated every new book Mayre read in class because I wanted her to LOVE READING. She would diligently read through each book and proudly say, "Matha, don't you think we should celebrate tonight."*
> *The next year I celebrated after every five books completed. Now Mayre so loves to read that she will often give up her half hour TV time to read. Celebrating Mayre's small reading successes definitely helped her value reading and encouraged her to become a more successful Super Star reader.*

All dressed up and smiling to celebrate her first Gold Medal.

2. Celebrating Can Be Simple and Cost Effective

First we start with our celebration song: "Celebrate, Celebrate, Dance to the Music" (The Three Dog Night Song—
"Celebrate"). The key is to jump up and down and swing
round and round as you sing those words:

*Celebrate, Celebrate, Dance to the Music . . . My Mayre
completed her first reading book . . . is an accomplished*

> *Math Wizard . . . played her own piano composition . . .*
> *(announce the accomplishment over and over).*

Then, since Mayre and I are alone at home, I usually walk to the front door, open the door and yell out to the neighborhood, or if I am in the car I roll down the window and yell,

> *"Hear Ye, Hear Ye...My daughter Mayre G. Mulvaney just completed her first reading book. I am very proud of her. Let's give her a round of applause."* Then I wildly APPLAUD. **Applause is the single biggest motivator of children—applaud your children often.**

Of course, I am yelling into the wind. No one is listening, but Mayre doubles over in wits of laughter every time, even though she knows I am preparing to do this. Once again, as your children age you might change your antics, but I will probably do this even when Mayre is an adult.

3. Include Your Family

Family is important to us, so I usually pick up the phone and call my mother, sister, and brother in Maryland, even though we live in Arizona. Upon hearing the particular Mayre accomplishment, they hoot and holler and make it a big deal.

> **The total cost:** The cost of the phone calls to Maryland from Arizona.
>
> **The total time involved:** Less than 20 minutes.
>
> **The result:** A child excited about her accomplishments.

4. Big-Time Celebrating

> ☆ **Go to your Celebration Station.** Since I rarely take Mayre to fast food establishments like MacDonald's, Dairy Queen, or Burger King, she loves to go to our Celebration Station at one of these places. Of course, if you frequent these places regularly, then your child will

say, "No Big Deal!" My suggestion . . . stop going so often and save these for special events and celebrations.

☆ **Put signs all over the front or back yard.** If you don't have a front yard or a back yard, make signs and put them all over the house, all over the child's bedroom, or in her lunch box or backpack. The point is to Acknowledge, Acknowledge, and Acknowledge!

> **My child is Bright!**

> **Yeah, Mayre!**

> **She just completed her multiplication tables!**

All you need is a bin of paper that you are recycling, or the end of fax rolls, a basket of magic markers, and a vivid imagination. I am not a particularly good artist, but I can print and use various colors. You don't have to make it perfect—just make it.

☆ **Go to your favorite restaurant**—not a fast food place. At your favorite family home-style restaurant or fancy restaurant, ask the waitress or waiter to bring something special for YOUR LITTLE SUPER STAR. Explain your child's accomplishment. Tell the waitress you think that a super star like this deserves something special. Nine times out of ten the waitress or waiter is more than willing to bring out a special dessert or treat. If they choose not to assist in your celebration, then take your business elsewhere. Of course, do not continually go back to the same place or they will think you are a mooch. Spread the joy around and frequent many different places.

☆ **Celebrate your child's birthday with acknowledgment of who she or he is.** Instead of the usual ice cream and cake, I take time to go to Mayre's school and acknowledge her. I bring photo albums of her orphanage in Vietnam. I tell the class how exciting it was to live with 26 other little children and be able to play and run all day long. I tell of the caretakers who adored her and the family that sacrificed so she would be adopted and come to America. I celebrate her gold medals and piano awards. Mayre always listens intently, with the other children, enthralled by her own story. If the class has a video, I play clips of "Mayre Movies."

I celebrate Mayre's adoption. Children can be cruel. They have said cruel things to Mayre about being adopted until I started celebrating her birthday and her adoption. By the time I finish, most of the kids wish they had been adopted too.

**Celebration doesn't have to be elaborate.
You just have to remember to do it!**

Exercise:

List all of your family's major celebrations.

Think of ways to involve your children in planning the celebrations.

List accomplishments to celebrate for each child. Remember, very young children, or children with challenges and difficulties may need many small occasions to celebrate to improve their self-esteem.

Celebrate, Celebrate, Mayre graduates from Kindergarten.

Insights and Notes

15

Create Opportunities for Success

In college, repeatedly I was told, *Students need at least 100 repetitions to learn a new skills. A student with challenges needs at least 500 repetitions.*

Mayre had come to me with many challenges—hearing loss, poor self-esteem and few skills. My goal was to provide her with as many small successes as humanly possible. Setting children up for success is very instrumental in helping them become Super Stars. Children with high self-esteem think they can do anything—and they can. Create opportunities for success . . . do not leave it to chance.

CONTESTS

Contests give children an opportunity to succeed at all ages. Contests are not just about winning or losing, although that can be an extra added benefit. Contests are about completing a task to the best of your ability, meeting a deadline, and celebrating the feeling of success that comes from the process of completing a task.

While walking through our PetsMart store, Mayre (age four then) spied a poster with a pocket containing coloring papers. The sign said, "Enter the PetsMart coloring contest and win prizes. All entries must be completed by Friday."

We took the entry form home. I explained:

Many children will take a form home. Each child who completes the picture by Friday will have a chance to win the prizes. All I ask is that you do the best job you can and complete this paper by Thursday so we can turn it in to the PetsMart manager early.

The contest was a great way to help Mayre understand the importance of completing a project to the best of her ability and meeting a deadline. Mayre diligently worked on her coloring paper. When she completed the paper she brought it to me and said, "This is my best work." Although her coloring went outside the lines and looked a little wild, she had completed the task.

I presented Mayre with a Super Star sticker. I explained, "Completing the task shows Mom you are a Super Star. Although I would love you to win the contest, you are already a winner in Mom's eyes." Whether Mayre won or lost was minor compared to the success she felt in completing the task. We celebrated her timely completion of the project!

On Saturday, we took a trip to PetsMart to see the results of the contest. Mayre had won in her age category. She proudly went to the manager's office and asked if she could have her prizes. The manager announced over the loud speaker, "We have a winner in the store. Our four year old contest winner, Mayre G. Mulvaney, just won our store's prizes. Let's give her a round of applause." The whole store started cheering.

The manager pulled me aside before we departed and said, "Mayre was the only child under seven who completed the coloring paper." I grinned from ear to ear. She had won because she had completed the task. What a great lesson for Mayre! She won and she felt like a winner.

The exercise taught her completing a task to the best of your ability is one of the secrets to becoming a successful Super Star.

Mayre was hooked on contests after that. She entered store contests, radio station contests, and even TV contests. Each time she completed the task, we celebrated. Then came an essay contest in kindergarten. The contest was presented at Arizona State University for the Grand Canyon State Games sponsored by Ottawa University. Mayre brought the entry form home from school and immediately we sat down and brain stormed. She then began writing her essay. She wrote and rewrote her essay until she was satisfied she had done the best she could do. Mayre won a Bronze Medal and was invited to a huge celebration with sports heroes and local news people.

Throughout our home, I have placed our family motto:

If you believe it in your heart,
see it in your mind's eye,
and take action,
you can bring anything to pass.

By first grade Mayre couldn't wait to enter again. The topic was "A LESSON I LEARNED FROM SPORTS." Once again, we brain stormed and Mayre started writing. She wrote about her sports heroine, Kerri Strug. The huge number of entrants had overwhelmed the selection committee. The contest was gaining popularity. Mayre was anxious to hear the results.

Yes . . . She won the Gold medal!

Mayre's essay so impressed the committee they contacted Kerri Strug. Mayre had dreamed about meeting Kerri Strug, her Olympic heroine. She **believed she could** meet her one day; she **visualized she would** meet her one day; and she **took action** to meet her Kerri. You can imagine Mayre's excitement when the committee called to announce

Kerri Strug would be in Phoenix to present the medals to all the children at the Grand Canyon State Games. Even more exciting, Mayre was the only child invited, as a special guest, to have dinner with Kerri and her family. The local news media put the story on TV.

Kerri Strug, Olympic Gold Medallist, and Mayre, Gold Medal Essay Winner.

A Lesson in Life I Learned From Sports ... Caring For Others With A Brave Heart

by Mayre G. Mulvaney

It all started when my mom and I sat down to watch the Atlanta Olympics. There I met my heroine, Kerrie Strug. Kerri is a gymnast. I admire Kerri because she supported her teammates.

When it was their turn, Kerrie clapped and cheered. "Go! Go! Go!" But the lesson of life I learned from watching Kerri was caring for other people.

Kerri was preparing to have her turn on the vault. Even though she was injured, she leaped into the air and completed her turn. She landed with her head high and hands in the air. Everyone in the whole world was clapping. Do you know why she took her turn? Well, she was helping her team win.

She didn't think "Me, me, me." She thought, "How can I help, help, help my team?"

I'm now in gymnastics and my teacher taught me the same----to support and help, help, help other people on my team. I'm going to be in the Olympics when I grow up. I'll cooperate with my team mates and we'll win. Every one knew Kerri was in pain. Many wanted Kerrie to stop. But Kerri did what was in her heart, not what everyone else thought she should do. She became a true champion, even though she didn't get a gold medal. I would like to be just like Kerri Strug----a true champion with a brave heart and a helping hand for others. While I'm in school, I'll help my friends and gymnastics teammates whenever they need help. When I grow up, I'm going to be a doctor and care for all the people that are my patients. Caring for other people is important in sports and also in all my life.

☆ **Contests provide small successes** that build and build to large successes.

☆ **Concentrate your child's efforts** on enjoying the success that comes from completing a task to the best of her ability. When you enjoy the task and complete the task the natural outgrowth is winning.

> *If you believe it in your heart,*
> *see it in your mind's eye,*
> *and take action,*
> *you can bring anything to pass.*

LETTER WRITING TO NATIONAL PERSONALITIES

As I have previously mentioned, we enjoy discussing all kinds of topics at dinner. We had discussed Mrs. Clinton's book, *It Takes a Village*. Mayre then saw the First Lady on TV. She decided Mrs. Hillary Clinton was a good mommy to

Chelsea, and she wanted to meet the First Lady. I suggested Mayre write Mrs. Clinton a letter and tell her so.

Mayre wrote to Mrs. Clinton and I mailed the letter to 1600 Pennsylvania Ave. Two weeks later, Mayre received a response from the White House. How gracious of Mrs. Clinton and her staff to respond so quickly. Mayre took the envelope, letter and picture of Mrs. Clinton to her first grade class for show and tell. Of course, Mayre has not given up her dream of meeting Mrs. Clinton one day; but already she knows the power of taking action to bring your dreams to fruition.

Another personality that Mayre became enamored with was Rosie O' Donnell. Mayre was thrilled that Rosie had an adoptive son named Parker. She felt connected to Rosie. Mayre wanted to be on the "Kids Joke Section" of Rosie's show or perform with John, Rosie's orchestra leader, on the piano.

Mayre wrote Rosie almost daily. No response. After twenty attempts it became apparent Mayre was not going to get a response. We happened to have an upcoming trip to New York City. I called ahead—no tickets to the show. We even tried to get tickets once in New York, but to no avail. The Rosie show had limited seating and was very popular.

Not always do children have as much success as Mayre had with writing to Mrs. Clinton. Rather than have Mayre become discouraged, I created a way for her to feel successful so she would continue to take action to make her dreams come true. On one of my many flights, I sat next to Linda Caffarello. One thing led to another, and I disclosed how Mayre had written so often to Rosie. Linda had been to the Rosie show and she said she would help keep Mayre encouraged.

A week later, Mayre received an envelope addressed to her. She tore it open and found Rosie O'Donnell stuff inside. She was so excited because she thought her TV pal, Rosie, had sent her the presents. Mayre immediately wrote and thanked Rosie, *"You see dreams do come true with Rosie."* Of course, Linda Caffarello sent the items. Thank you Linda, where ever you are! You encouraged Mayre to continue taking action toward her dreams. Mayre and I still love Rosie, and maybe one day we'll get to meet her.

☆ Letter writing provides small successes that build and build to large successes.

☆ When your children are young, create successful outcomes. Your children will build high self-esteem that will serve them well when they experience disappointments.

☆ Concentrate your children's efforts on enjoying the success that comes from taking action to make their dreams come true. Enjoy the process no matter what the outcome.

If you believe it in your heart,
see it in your mind's eye,
and take action,
you can bring anything to pass.

CREATE A SUPER STAR ATMOSPHERE

Whatever your child's talent, provide him or her with as many small successes as possible. When Mayre showed interest in music, I started to create a musical environment. I collected toy instruments, real instruments and musical games. Every night after dinner we would play a musical game. It was difficult to locate many musical games so we used regular board games and improvised.

☆ **Applaud attempts**—Any attempt Mayre made in the direction of the musical instruments met with applause. *That was a great song you just made up on your toy saxophone. You are really talented in music.*

☆ **Enjoy the process**—Having fun with the instruments created excitement. I interacted with Mayre while playing the instruments.
I'll play the drums while you create a masterpiece on the piano.

☆ **Make a Big Star on a piece of paper.** Have your child create pictures or words that describe him or her as a SUPER STAR and place the pictures and words inside the star.

I AM A SUPER STAR!

My sister, Susan, who is exceptionally gifted in the crafts area, created a beautiful mirror for Mayre that had "I AM A WINNER!" painted around the frame. Every day Mayre looks at herself and says, "I am a Winner. I am a Super Star!

☆ **Use positive Attitude Technologies with your child.**

If you believe it in your heart,
see it in your mind's eye,
and take action,
you can bring anything to pass.

If your children only have disappointments from the beginning, they expect disappointments and never try. They begin to believe life is too hard, meeting their hero is not possible, and they have no control over life.

If you create an atmosphere where your child has many successes, it builds self-esteem. With high self-esteem your Super Star can do anything—including handle disappointments. Your Super Star will take risks and take action to make his or her dreams come true. Teach and encourage the Attitude Technology:

If you believe it in your heart,
see it in your mind's eye,
and take action,
you can bring anything to pass.

Uncle Dennis, Auntie Susan, Winston (the dog) and Mayre. Thanks Auntie for the mirror . . . I am a winner!

Insights and Notes

16

Make Mealtime Creative

Mealtime always brings back fond memories. Not just because my mom was a great cook, but because mealtimes were great fun. I remember, as an adult, bringing a friend over for dinner. This woman sat with her mouth open as she watched everyone excitedly talking at once. When mother asked her opinion of the topic at hand, the woman replied, "Which one? ya'll have five different topics going on at once." We all laughed as we saw it from her point of view. She had grown up in a household where children were seen but not heard. Dinner time was for eating and watching TV, not talking. There was no conversation at her dinner table except father telling everyone how his day had gone. So we sounded pretty raucous to her.

PLAN A PLEASANT MEALTIME

Most families I know today do not eat together. If they do eat together it is with the TV blasting. There is little conversation and everyone flies to the next event as soon as they have gulped down the food.

Turn Off the TV and Talk

I know, NO TV is a novel concept in America, but it works. Besides, isn't that what VCRs were invented for—to record shows that you missed but would like to watch at a later time? I don't know how to stop the 12:00 from blinking but I do know how to record a show. Record it and talk for a change.

Mayre's second grade class was asked to turn off TV, Game Boys, and other electronic games for one week. Each child who could make it just one week without electronics won $50 worth of Class Bucks to purchase class prizes. Mayre and one other child were the only two children in the entire class to make it through one week. When the teacher asked, "What happened?" the students responded, "How could anyone last a week without TV or Game Boy?" or "My parents said it would be okay to watch just a little TV." I thought that was so sad.

If you are one of those people who just could not possibly turn off the TV, then at least use it to your advantage. Ask questions about the shows to see if your children understood what they watched.

Children need time to use their verbal skills. If they do not use these skills they lose these skills. Create an atmosphere where they feel safe to share thoughts and ideas and are encouraged to do so.

Set Dinnertime Sharing Rules

☆ Every person at the table gets to share an idea or something he or she wants to share.

☆ Each night, a different person is chosen to start.

☆ Every person must listen first before getting an opportunity to speak. Those who do not respect and listen to the person speaking lose their turn to share and can try again the next night.

☆ If you do not have something to share, which was rare in our house, you can use sentence starters and ask each child to finish them.

Sentence Starters

If you were a fruit, an animal, a flower, a car, a house, an insect . . . what would you be?

If you could have any mother or father in the whole world to include movie stars . . . who would you pick? (Of course, that was always a trick question because we would pick our own mom and dad, which always brought a smile to my mom's face.)

If you could be President for a day, what would you change in America?

Who is your favorite character from history and why?

If you were the Statue of Liberty, what would you say to the people coming to America?

Name two things you learned at school today. Name two things your learned from the newspaper or TV news.

Name one accomplishment from today that you are most proud. Name one thing you did today that you would have done differently.

Name one wise choice you made today. Name one poor choice you made today, and tell what you could have done differently.

What do you think about . . . politics, the president, the weather, the senate race . . . questions that call for an opinion. (Remember the rules, respect each other. If you do not agree with a family team member you say, "You are entitled to your opinion but mine differs from yours." You may not say, "That is the stupidest thing I have ever heard. What are you—brain dead!" Such comments are banished and if they pop up, the person loses a turn or is asked to speak in a more appropriate manner.)

If children never get to practice polite dinner conversation, they do not learn it. LET YOUR CHILDREN PRACTICE, PRACTICE, PRACTICE to be Super Star Conversationalists.

Use Positive Spaced Repetition Mealtime Statements

One of my favorite audiences, to whom I speak, is School Food Service (the school lunch room personnel). I am convinced they can really make a difference in our schools. They see almost every child, teacher, and administrator each and every day. I continually help them understand that they can raise the IQ of America if they will use positive spaced repetition in the nation's cafeterias.

Remember when you were a child. What were your two favorite subjects? . . . recess and lunch, right. When I went to school, the only things we had to watch out for was running in the halls, chewing gum in class, spit balls, and shirt tails out. Nowadays, our children are confronted with assault, theft, robbery, abuse (physical, sexual, and mental), and school bombings. Many of our students don't want to go to recess or lunch because it can be scary.

It's time to bring back our favorite subject—lunch—by creating a fun and exciting dining experience. I often ask the lunch room staff to do the following activities with the children. Parents can do the same activities at home.

Use 3x5 cards to encourage

The first month of school, every lunch tray should have a 3x5 card attached in the corner that says:

I AM A SUPER STAR! I AM A WINNER!

Always write your positive statements in the present, not I would like to some day be a Super Star, but I AM a Super Star. Each month change the 3x5 card to the next expectation.

2nd month   I AM A WELL-BEHAVED SUPER STAR!

3rd month I AM A BRIGHT SUPER STAR!

4th month I AM A HEALTHY SUPER STAR! I MAKE
WISE FOOD CHOICES!

5th month I AM A CONFIDENT SUPER STAR!

6th month I AM A HAPPY SUPER STAR!

Encourage the behaviors you would like to see increase. Parents please use these same techniques at home for meal times, they work!

As each student comes through the lunch line have the staff make encouraging comments pertaining to the 3x5 card of the month:

It's great to see such a super star.
Thank you for being in my lunch line.
Come back tomorrow.
I can't wait to see your super star face again.

2nd month:

What a well behaved group.
It is a pleasure to serve such well-behaved children.
Thank you for being in my lunch line.
Come back tomorrow.

So on and so on.

CREATE A FUN ENVIRONMENT

Humor helps students do better on tests, according to a San Diego State study.

Make mealtime fun
Make 'em laugh
Make 'em Laugh, Make 'em Laugh

Recently, I spoke for PMG, a school lunch management firm in New Jersey. For years I have opposed management firms in our school lunch programs until I met the gang from PMG. If this company ran all our school cafeterias, we would have better cafeterias and students would love lunch time again.

PMG's philosophy is "We are here to serve our customers, and our customers are kids." Every one I met, from the president to the front line employees, displayed extraordinary customer service for kids.

The meeting I attended was a "LOVE BOAT" theme— "Cruisin' into the New Millennium." The president of the company arrived in a Captain Stubing uniform, and his entire staff was in nautical attire. The company created a cruise ship atmosphere to include photos of each attendee as they entered the Love Boat, a cruise ship yummy buffet luncheon, and free gifts for everyone. The president and his staff were there to serve the school cafeteria personnel, and they did. Their philosophy:

We treat you the way we would like you to treat the customer—our children.

The communication I heard again and again throughout the day was "create a fun environment for all cafeterias." Hire employees who have a sense of humor and love children. Decorate your cafeterias with everything from happy signs and balloons to inflatable rafts that become ice coolers. Create themes around certain times of the year or to coordinate with learning themes in the school . . . Under the Sea, Cruisin' into Science week, or to create excitement about certain foods . . . a broccoli bonanza, carrot cartoons, veggie variety etc. Transform your cafeterias into fun learning environments and the students will literally eat it up.

Mealtime can be a wonderful adventure into learning and setting positive attitudes. Do everything you can to create Super Star mealtimes.

Exercise:
Customize your own family mealtime plan. Ask each member of the family to contribute a suggestion.

Insights and Notes

Girls just "wanna" have fun (Auntie Susan, Maureen, Marie and Mayre).

16

 Select the Proper
Learning Environment
for Your Super Star

Can you image buying a new car by just walking into a dealership and saying, "Wrap it up, I'll take it." Wouldn't you at least kick the tires, ask what was under the hood, and look at the gas mileage criteria? Yet most of us continue to allow our children to walk in and attend school without question.

It's time to kick the tires of education. Up until a few years ago, public schools and private schools were our only choices. Most private schools were so expensive, we could not even consider them as a viable option. Not so nowadays! We have more choices because parents are demanding more choices. We have public schools, which now include charter schools and other varieties of free public education. We have private schools, private combined with public, and home schools. Parents can now choose the most appropriate learning environment for their children.

When choosing a school for Mayre, I visited every school, public and private, within a 25 mile radius of my home. I wanted to ensure that Mayre would be in a learning environment conducive to our family values. Although I would have loved to home school, Mayre came from an orphanage. She does much better in group situations than in solitary situations. Choose what is best for your child.

CHOOSING THE RIGHT SCHOOL FOR YOUR CHILD

Go to Each School in Your Surrounding Area and Observe

To cut down on the amount of time spent, I gathered six other sets of parents. We divided our geographic area and asked each set of parents to go to different schools. The parents reported back to the group about their experience with their school. We narrowed down our selections to three different schools and asked each parent to personally observe that school.

Stand in the School and Ask Yourself How It Feels to You

I know you are saying, " That sounds very touchy-feelie," but it works. Even our men parents came back and said, "I felt uneasy in school number one. It felt chaotic to me. I couldn't concentrate. In school number three I felt calm and peaceful. I felt happy."

How you feel is exactly how your child will feel because they usually have your value system. Pay attention to the feeling in the school.

Ask Questions!

Here are some questions we used when selecting a school:

What is your philosophy of education? What is your school's vision?

How will your school assist my child to become the best he or she can be? What self-concept building strategies does your school have in place?

What are the positive discipline strategies for your school?

How will I be informed of the progress of my child?

What systems do you have so I may communicate effectively with the teacher or administrative staff?

At one of the schools I visited, I asked the teacher, "If I have a challenge with something, may I call you to clarify or get a better understanding?"

The teacher said, "I do not get paid to take phone calls from parents, just write me a note and I'll see what I can do." Needless to say, I canceled this school completely off the list.

As an administrator, what is your management style with your teachers? (Most teachers will treat students the way they are treated! When teachers are treated with respect and dignity they will treat students with respect and dignity.)

What kind of teacher training do your teachers receive each year? Are they trained in positive coaching and motivation techniques? How often do teachers get recertified and what is the process?

Exercise

Make your own list of questions that relate to your values.

BE CREATIVE

My first hurdle was to locate the best learning environment for my daughter. The second hurdle was how to get there. I could not car pool because of my busy schedule, and there was no bus system. Instead of giving up on the school of choice, I got creative. When your children see you solve challenges, they learn to solve challenges as well.

The Challenge:

Come up with a way to transport my daughter and five other children to the school one half hour from our home.

The Solution:

Create our own bus system. I called every transport system from airport shuttles to taxis. We asked for bids, collected data, and created a wonderful bus system. The children enjoyed getting to know each other and have bus play time. The parents formed a deep and lasting bond, and we all enjoyed having a safety net of five other sets of parents willing and able to help in any emergency situation.

As a single parent, with no relatives in my immediate area, I must be creative. Once again I looked to the business community for a model. Most corporations are now seeking partnershiping opportunities. Hospitals partnership with past competitor hospitals to share multi-million dollar equipment. They want to leverage time and money by sharing equipment, personnel, and ideas.

I needed to create partnershiping opportunities to leverage my time, money, and ideas. Although I live in the Wild Wild West and we still believe in being neighborly, it takes effort to be neighborly.

Make the effort to form small parent groups. By asking six family units to come together, we were able to create the money to attract a driver and a bus. By meeting at a nearby park for pick up and drop off, we were able to leverage our time. By forming the "bus group," we developed friendships that helped teach our children the importance of friendships. Friendships are very important to create a sense of community. We learn to depend on each other. My adult bus friends assist me with Mayre when I go out of town and they depend on me to assist them with their children. We are modeling sharing, connectedness, friendship, leadership skills, and partnershiping.

EMPOWER YOUR CHILDREN

There will be many situations in which you cannot be around to protect and shelter your child. If you march into school each time your child is teased or picked on, you will teach your child that she isn't good enough, strong enough, or smart enough to take care of herself. You must teach your child strategies to empower her (Of course if your child is in eminent physical or emotional danger, take action and step in).

The neighborhood children often tormented my mom. She developed many strategies that she passed on to us.

Humor

I was continually teased for having red hair and massive amounts of freckles. The other children would chant, "I'd rather be dead than red in the head" or "freckle face hang your head in disgrace." Inevitably, I would be in tears when I got home. My mother would tell me the freckles were kisses from God and the other kids were just jealous because they didn't have freckles. My standard reply was, "They can have mine."

Ignore and Distract

Mother would say,

> I can go in and talk to your teacher, but then the children will just pick on you all the more. The more you react, the more they will tease. The best thing to do is "ignore and distract." It is very hard to continue picking on someone who is not reacting and who is laughing. When the kids tease you say, "That's not very funny, but did

you hear this one," and tell a joke." or "Talk to the hand
because the ears can't hear." It worked most of the time.

Send Negative Energy Back to Its Source

I shared the following technique with Mayre; it really
works!

I put on my "positive space suit" every day before I leave
the house. Any time someone says something positive to
me, it is allowed in. Any time someone says something
negative to me, it bounces right off my positive space suit
right back to the source.

State Your Feelings and Ask for Change

Mayre came home in tears one day. A child, twice her size,
was picking on her. Mayre had befriended this child because
she had no other friends. Because Mayre was her only
friend, every time this child got angry she lashed out at
Mayre. We tried the humor and it worked for a few weeks.
Then we had to learn more strategies.

Mayre said, "Joan (not her real name) called me a jerk. I
said I'm telling my mother on you." Joan replied, "You have
to tell your mother because you don't even have a father!"
Mayre sobbed, "That really hurt my feelings."

Now as a mother, I felt as if someone had put a dagger
right in my heart. I wanted to go in and rip this little child's
face off. But instead I talked to Mayre quietly.

I asked Mayre, Would you ever think to say something
so mean to another child?

No, Mom, I would never have even thought to say some-
thing that mean. It would not have crossed my mind."

First, look at what the person said and take it apart

It sure would not have crossed my mind either. So it
dawns on me that this must be something about Joan's

father and she is taking it on you. When people say such mean things it often means something is going on in their own lives. I remember you telling me that Joan's father does not live with them—maybe she misses her dad. Maybe she is angry with him for leaving and she is taking it out on you.

If it is not true, then do not accept it

She said you don't have a father. DUH . . . you have a father, in Vietnam. He just does not live with us. So that is not true.

Use the "I mean it" voice

Tell Joan that she hurt your feelings and you would appreciate her not saying that to you again. Say it in a clear, strong, I MEAN IT voice.

Mayre went back to school and talked to her friend. This worked for quite a while.

Give Warning—Cut Off Relationship

Then Mayre came home again in tears, "Joan said that I'm stupid because I'm Vietnamese."

We went through the process again.

How could that be true—you are in second grade reading on a seventh grade level. Little Ms. Joan is not telling the truth, and she said that just to hurt and annoy you. It worked, you got annoyed.

This time say, "Joan I like you very much, but you continue to hurt my feelings on purpose. Please don't say mean things to me. If you are angry tell the teacher, but please do not take out your anger on me. If you continue to do this I will have to stop playing with you. This is my last warning."

Joan said something mean and Mayre choose to steer clear of Joan for a whole week.

Use Your Brains Not Your Fists

Several weeks later things heated up again. Joan had again picked on Mayre at recess. Joan had pulled Mayre's hair and hit her in the back. Mayre had hauled off and socked Joan back. The teacher had seen only what Mayre did and had taken away Mayre's privileges. Mayre said, "I didn't want to hit her but I had no choice. It is unfair that the teacher punished me and not her."

"You are right, life is unfair," I said. "Sometimes the teacher does not know the source of the problem. She saw you sock Joan and so you were blamed. That is unfortunate, but it does happen. I know you explained your side, but it was the wrong time and the teacher could not hear you effectively. Of course, mother never wants you to be abused in any way, but I also do not want you to use violence. Mulvaneys think their way out of problems."

You had many choices. **Let's explore the choices.**

1. You could have run away. You are the fastest kid in the class. Do you mean you could not run faster than Joan?

2. You could have scared Joan by saying, STOP very loudly.

3. You could have done a wrestling move by falling to the floor and feigning pain so Joan would have been the person the teacher punished instead of you.

4. You could have asked for a conference with your teacher before the problem escalated to this level. I do not want you to be a tattletale, but I also want you to know when it is appropriate time to ask for help. This fight did not just start on the playground, it started in class, correct?

5. You could have written a note to the teacher that you were in trouble.

6. You could have spit and foamed at the mouth. Certainly someone would have come over then.

Mayre you had many options. Since you chose violence, you suffered the consequences of being blamed. Let's remember Mayre, you could really hurt someone using your fists. You go to a personal trainer with Mom and you do weight training. How would you have felt if you had really hurt Joan? Which of the above choices would have been a wiser choice?

Do Not Fight Your Child's Battles

If your super star never has to make choices, she does not develop confidence. If you condone violence, your child learns to solve problems with violence—which is the easiest way out of something. It can spiral out of control. Teach problem solving instead. Empower your child!

After a long discussion, Mayre chose to talk with her teacher, with Mom along for support. Mayre did the talking and explained she had tried various techniques and still Joan picked on her. She asked for support from the teacher and asked her to move her desk away from Joan. They set up a signal to warn the teacher if Mayre was being picked on. The teacher would then step over and engage Joan in another activity. Problem solved.

Mayre did the solving and she felt excited that she took charge of the situation. She now has many ways to solve a problem that she has tested herself. She knows that she can use words, humor, and support from teachers.

We all take licks in life, here and there. Teasing, as much as I would like to eradicate it, is part of living on planet earth. The skills necessary to solve the challenges surrounding teasing have to be taught. Teach these skills to your child. Your child has to practice these skills in youth to be better prepared as an adult. By stepping in or condoning violence "Just hit them back" where does it stop? I hit you with my fist and you hit me with a stick. I hit you back with a stick then you run home and get a gun. You shoot at me and I run home and make a bomb. Violence begets violence. Think your way out of a problem. Teach your child to be a Super-Star Problem Solver!

Insights and Notes

18

Select the Right Teacher for Your Super Star

Self-esteem is a better predictor of reading ability than IQ, according to The Wattenberg and Clifford Study. This means that no subject matter learning has ever suffered because of time spent on self-concept building. A San Diego State Study showed that humor helped students do better on tests.

A Wisconsin study revealed that when children enter first grade, 80% of them feel pretty good about themselves; but by the time they get to the sixth grade, only 10% of them have good a self-image. A national PTA study showed that in most American schools, 18 negative statements are identified for every positive statement.

My personal criteria for an outstanding teacher is someone *who walks their talk.* Since I take my job as a parent seriously, I expect the teachers of my Super Star to be just as committed. I seek teachers who are committed to developing and nurturing Super Stars instead of teachers who just teach. Make it your mission to find Super Star teachers.

Super Star Teacher—Heidi Jo Grimes
"Mrs. Heidi"

Mrs. Heidi with Mayre—Junior Original
Medallist.

Mayre's love of music began the minute she could hear.
Immediately, I bought a piano when Mayre was age three so
she could experiment with sounds. A wonderful young man
named Mr. Karl, a Yamaha teacher, began teaching Mayre.
Having never heard of Yamaha, I assumed it was the school
Mr. Karl attended. It didn't matter, Mayre loved learning
with Mr. Karl because he was so fun. Suddenly, Mr. Karl
became ill and stopped teaching.

We went through a succession of teachers to find the right fit for Mayre. Each of these teachers taught the way I had learned as a child. The teacher would present the lesson book and a few hints, the child was expected to play three songs by the next week, the mom had to teach the songs at home while cajoling, bribing or coaxing the child to practice. The whole scenario started again the next week. Mayre had loved playing piano with Mr. Karl but now she had an aversion to playing at all. I knew I had to take action and called Mr. Karl for a referral. He informed me that Yamaha was a method of teaching piano— not his alma mater, and that I should find a "Yamaha Teacher."

Immediately, I located the East Valley Yamaha Music School owned and directed by Mrs. Heidi. We made an

Mayre playing her original composition .

appointment for a trial group lesson. Upon entering the school's waiting room, I felt joyous and happy. Each parent in the waiting room excitedly told us good things about the school and Mrs. Heidi. The moment Mayre and I walked into the group, I knew I had found the right school and the right teacher for Mayre.

All 12 children were laughing and enjoying the piano. They sang a little, danced a little, and played the piano a little. All the parents were sitting behind the children and they too were asked to sing, dance, and play piano. The learning environment was contagious—no competition, just praise and encouragement for each child who attempted to play, and every child attempted to play! The children encouraged each other, "Come on Jennifer, you can do it." The parents clapped for each and every child. This school and this teacher were aligned with the Mulvaney Family Vision—encouragement, encouragement, encouragement. I enrolled on the spot.

Mrs. Heidi is one of the most gifted teachers I have ever had the privilege to know. Mayre has excelled under her tutelage. Mrs. Heidi made my Super Star Teacher List! I thought it important to feature her in this book.

I asked her: "What made you the teacher and parent you are today? What lessons would you like to share with others so they, too, can raise Super Stars?"

Mrs. Heidi joyfully told me, "I am the teacher I am today because of my family. I was one of 11 children. My parents always encouraged my siblings and me to find our special gift, develop it, and use it to benefit others. We weren't just encouraged by words but by the actions of our parents. My father, a physician, and my mother, a nurse, modeled their special gifts as medical missionaries. My family traveled around the world from England to Tanzania as my parents helped others. We eventually settled in Minnesota on a farm.

Every child was encouraged to take piano lessons and learn one other instrument. Our home library almost surpassed the rural public library because it was so extensive. Mealtimes were discussion times. We often had heated debates over books, philosophies, and every other subject in between.

I felt my parents' approval and encouragement strongly as a child. Once I was making a cake and I spilled the flour all over the floor and was quite upset. My mother just began to laugh. As I went to clean it up, Mother said, "No, leave it." Then she got down on all fours and we began to make beautiful pictures in the flour. The excitement, support, and people skills I gained from being one of many siblings has proved a benefit in my adult life as a teacher and mother.

As long as I can remember I wanted to be a teacher. My life was changed when, in college, I watched a presentation of the Yamaha Education System and knew that was the teaching vehicle for me.

The traditional piano private lesson style teaching, that is so prevalent in the U.S.A., did not seem to fit my background. But Yamaha was perfect. Lessons are taught in small groups with parental involvement. The teachers are given unequaled teaching techniques and materials. The Yamaha philosophy is to teach the language of music using piano and keyboards as the tool. To this end, they use ear training, harmony, solfege, rhythm training, music reading, ensemble, and most importantly improvisation and composition. The students' self-esteem soars.

My classes are places of cooperation not competition. The parents applaud the achievements of all the students. The students work as teams to improvise, sing in parts, and play ensembles. This reliance on one another and the resulting performances in class, are pure joy when everyone is sensitive to each other and the music. Also, I highly encourage discovery. I want the students and my children to express their opinions and display their creativity.

Music is a tool to open the soul. In class, that openness is vital to achieve solo and ensemble performances. When children compose, they show the depth to which they've integrated their musical skills, and it is the most comprehensive level of musical understanding. Each year, we have a Junior Original Concert. These are special concerts at the local, regional, national, and international levels. This unique program encourages and trains young musicians to compose their own music. It validates their hard work and creativity, unlike any other music festival or competition for young children.

MRS. HEIDI'S TECHNIQUES AND ATTITUDES

As a teacher who has watched hundreds of parents with their children and now is blessed with four of my own, these are some of the techniques and attitudes that make a difference in my classes and in my home.

A Positive I Can, You Can Attitude

The Bible says, "A pleasant teacher is best!" I never have a "bad" day at teaching.

Really Loving My Children and Students—Every One!

I never let myself consider a negative emotion towards students. They are all my favorites. Children can read adult emotions. They know when you favor one over the other. When I see young students, I see the special abilities or strengths they have, and as a teacher I automatically see what they might become. I treat them as the gifted musicians I see. I watch for the moments of opportunity when they are able to absorb a new concept or move to a new level of difficulty. When I teach, the students are part teacher, showing me the next step to lead them to. I never limit them or give up on them!

Using the 3 Rs—Respond, Respect and Restrict

Children are biologic learners. Adults are logic learners. A child learns from experience, experimentation, curiosity, and free exploration. Adults learn from studying, reading, and mental analysis.

Look at a typewriter. You know that if you push the "Y" key a "Y" will be printed on the paper. You've reasoned it out. You don't have to push the "Y" key to know it will cause the typewriter to print the letter "Y" on the paper.

Your child, on the other hand, will look at the typewriter and push the "Y" key just to see what happens. When the "Y" appears on the paper, the child sees the effect . . . and with enough repetition the child learns that pushing the "Y" key creates a "Y" on the paper. This is the critical difference between the way adults learn and the way children learn.

The "THREE Rs" encourage us to remember and regard this difference—for the fullest benefit to every child's learning.

#1 R—Respond

I request all parents respond to the music for themselves rather than for the child. Get into the music yourself. Each child needs to be free to respond to the music the way he or she "feels" it—not the way you want him or her to respond. Only through this freedom of response can your child learn—often by trail and error—the world of music.

#2 R—Respect

Respect is allowing your child to respond in the physical (biologic) way, which is the way he or she is compelled to learn, instead of imposing the adult (logic) way to learn.

Watch and listen for how your child learns. Your child tries and imitates . . . tries and imitates . . . that's the true developmental learning process. To fully develop sensory-motor coordination, your child needs to have *many successful repetitions* of physical patterning before he or she can be expected to label the patterns or explain why he or she is doing it that way. If you interrupt your child's physical concentration with intellectual questioning, you deprive your child of his or her best learning tool.

#3R—Restrict

I ask parents to restrict adult chatter so the child can concentrate. The highest priority in musical training is listening. If parents talk during ear training sessions, they interfere with the child's ability to hear this new language and to acquire the necessary motor skills to sing and play it.

At times, it will seem easier for parents to explain the teacher's instructions than to let children learn on their own. But, remember, we want children to learn to trust their own ears, so they become musically independent.

I Involve My Children in My Life.

As a mother of four (ages 2, 4, 6, 8), I try to involve my children in my life as a teacher. Recently, our school increased in size so we had to move to larger surroundings. My children helped with the move, decorated the new settings, and delighted in their new "kids room" where they can read, relax, and wait for me to finish classes.

Coping as A Business Woman, Mother, Wife and Teacher

Time is precious. I have my house cleaned once a week. My cleaning lady is fabulous, and I can handle being busy because I know the lamp shades, window sills, and blinds are clean even if the playroom is covered with toys when I arrive home exhausted.

My husband helps with the cooking, laundry, and picking up. This wasn't always so—I had to let go of my expectations of the way he could accomplish these tasks. I'm thrilled when there are clean clothes, I just don't want to know what he mixed together in one load to get them clean.

I'm constantly finding ways to improve my parenting, my school, and my relationships. I never feel that I have "arrived," and there is always a new adventure on the horizon. I strive to be like my mom who works as a nurse, rides horses, and travels to Guatemala for medical mission trips. I strive to be like my dad who spent nine months in Antarctica as a physician at age 70. I strive to be like my 90 year old grandmother who drove across town to deliver my family Sunday dinner a week after our fourth child was born.

I agree with Maureen and the premise of this book—ALL CHILDREN ARE SUPER STARS! I want my four Super Stars to look at me and dream even bigger dreams than I had. I want my Super Stars to reach for their dreams with the full confidence of attaining them!

The Grimes Family: Tony, Heidi, Rachel, Josiah, Anna, Jessica—Super Stars All!

Super Star Teacher Shirin Bhaloo

Super Star teacher, Mrs. Shirin Bhaloo and Mayre.

Mrs. Shirin Bhaloo and Mrs. Jan Vickery founded the Ahwatukee Foothills Montessori Center on the belief that every child should be helped to reach his or her maximum potential and that every child has the right to be treated with love and respect in the school environment. The objectives were simple—to teach:

Joy of Learning   Self-Confidence

Self-Discipline   Concentration

Self-Motivation   Independence

Coordination   Orderly Work Habits

I spotted an article in the local paper about this school. The vision of the school fit the Mulvaney family values, so I moved to the next step: *Stand and Feel the Environment.* I felt calm, peaceful, and joyous—all at once.

Then I observed how the administration, Mrs. Bahloo and Mrs. Jan, treated the teachers. There was a real sense of equality and respect for all staff. They showed genuine care and concern for each other.

Next, I observed how the teachers and staff treated the children. Each and every teacher and staff member was respectful and courteous toward the children. They modeled every behavior they expected from the children. Mrs. Bhaloo demonstrated the proper way to get in line by getting in line herself. At one point, there was a need for Mrs. Bhaloo to cross in front of a child. Mrs. Bhaloo kindly said, "Excuse me, may I please cross in front of you?" The child responded courteously, "Yes, you may."

Finally, I observed the children. Every single child was engaged in purposeful work, either individually or cooperating with another child. The children were doing interesting and exciting work. When I asked how they liked the class one little boy piped up and said, "Did you know I can read. I'm only four years old and I can read. I just got my bookbag."

"What's a bookbag?" I asked.

"Here...see this is a bookbag. It lets everyone know you can read."

After endless hours of searching for the proper learning environment for Mayre's preschool, I had found a Super Star school with a Super Star teacher, Mrs. Bhaloo. Mayre attended the Ahwatukee Foothills Montessori Pre-school and Kindergarten from age three to age six. What a Super Star foundation she received.

I asked Mrs. Bhaloo: "What made you the teacher you are today? What lessons would you like to share with others so they, too, can raise Super Stars?" Mrs. Bhaloo'e eyes danced as she answered:

"I've wanted to be a teacher my whole life. My mother died when I was only eleven. My dear father influenced me tremendously. He highly valued education... "Remember, no one can take education away from you. Education is the key."

I was strongly influenced by an incident that happened right after my mother died. I failed an important class in school. Although I was an "A" student and ranked within the top five of the school, upon failure of this class I was placed in a situation where I either had to go into a vocational class or repeat the class. I knew I did not want to do manual labor the rest of my life, and I did not want the embarrassment of repeating the class, so I decided I would quit school.

My father had such a great sense of humor. Upon hearing my decision, he smiled as he gave me a choice, "Shirin you may either take the class again until you pass it, or I will carry you to school, every day on my back, until you pass the class. Which choice do you prefer?" Of course, I decided to repeat the class.

My father also valued kindness and peace. He left East India as a young man to make a better life for himself and his family in Africa. There were curfews for all the black people of our African town. Any black person caught out after curfew was severely beaten. Father could not bear to see a person beaten so he gave shelter and blankets when he could. His kindness impressed me greatly.

My sister and I both became teachers and directors of Montessori schools. My dream would be to have all the children of the world learn the Montessori way. Montessori teaches a hands-on approach, and the children learn self-discipline and self-worth. These are the building blocks to learning all the subject areas of reading, math, and so on.

Montessori children are not just students, they also become teachers and role models for each other. Montessori does not foster competition, we encourage children instead. We have children of different age levels and abilities combined. When a four year old learns to read, he is encouraged to progress to the next level because his five year old friend enjoys it so much. Reading comes easy for younger children and they want to learn. They often say, "I'm doing something others don't think I can do. I can read."

It was my vision for our school to combine learning subject areas with what I call a PEACE CURRICULUM. We cannot have peace on earth until we start teaching peaceful techniques. Here are some of the techniques we use at our school:

Gain New Information

Never stop learning yourself. Continuous learning for staff and teachers is paramount. We attend seminars and lectures on a regular basis to keep abreast of new ideas in the field. Learning new ideas and teaching strategies better enable teachers to stay fresh for students.

Attending Sister Jucenta's session on reading changed my attitude about reading. She said, "Reading is the key to the doors of knowledge. If you don't have the key, you'll never be able to enter the doors of knowledge." Reading is so important to build self-esteem. It is one of our school's foundation building blocks.

Model the Behavior You Expect

Respect must be earned. All staff members model the behaviors we expect from the children. We all use kind words, kind actions, and resolve challenges in a peaceful manner. We ask parents to also model the behaviors they expect. We discourage the use of fighting action toys, karate kicks and aggressive behaviors. Our environment is calm and peaceful.

Creative Visualization

Children close their eyes and create peaceful situations.

Sometimes we can see with our minds what we might not be able to see with our eyes. Look at the peaceful picture in your mind.

We use creative visualization in many ways. Sometimes the children visualize the stories we tell in class, or they might visualize a peaceful solution to a conflict they have been involved with. When they can see with their minds eye a different outcome, they can then work towards that new outcome.

Storytelling and Literature Based on Ethics

My dream was to create a peace curriculum. I wasn't sure exactly how to go about making this work in class until I went to a seminar by Sonny McFarlin. She gave us a list of books for children and adults that were based on ethics. (*See the book list for literature based on ethics in the Appendix.*) I lived in a small town and our bookstore did not carry some of these books. I had to drive 50 miles to get the first book on the list, *Something Special Within*. That book and the other books on the list were worth the drive. These books were instrumental in creating a peace course.

Every year I start my class with two books, *Something Special Within*, about inner peace, and *Black Elk Speaks*, living the road of peace, not conflict. I've become a storyteller weaving the lessons from these books through all of our daily activities.

One of the lessons from these books is that there are two roads in life.

☆ One road is the **Road of Difficulty**, which leads to conflicts, anger and chaos.

☆ The other road is the **Road to Peace**, which leads to joy, love and happiness.

There is a tree at the crossroad of these two paths. When we are on the peace path, the tree is nurtured by the Love light that shines from within and grows.

To make this concept come alive for the children, I bring in a tree, which we decorate daily with flowers, leaves, and beautiful doves. If you are on the "Road of Difficulty and Conflict," the birds won't fly to the tree, the flowers won't grow and the tree may wither and die. But if you are on the "Peace Path," the love light shines all around the tree and it thrives, survives, and flourishes. Which path should we choose for our class?

The impact of this story is incredible and carries into their lives. One of my parents came in and told me what had happened at their house right after this lesson. Little Mary had just come home from school. Mother was very upset about something that happened during the day. She was screaming, yelling, and behaving in a very angry manner.

Mary started to cry, "Mother please stop yelling. You will kill our peacetree."

The mother continued to rant and rave, dismissing Mary's plea.

Mary started to sob, "You don't understand Mother, the birds won't come, the flowers won't grow, and the tree will die. Please Mother, you must calm down and solve this problem peacefully or our tree will die."

"What are you talking about Mary, I'm not killing anything."

"Yes, you are. There are two roads in life, one of peace and one of difficulty. By being so angry and not solving your problem in a calm way, you are on the road of difficulty. Your love light doesn't shine when you are on that road. Our peace tree can only grow when you are on the path to peace.

You have to use kind words, respect and love. Please Mother, don't kill our tree!"

The mother finally got what Mary was telling her. She came in the next day and told me the story. She wanted to know if she too could sit in on my classes.

The Peaceful Process

Children must be taught peaceful ways to resolve conflicts. We teach the following peaceful process to resolve conflict.

State your feeling without blame

Teacher tells the child: You did something you shouldn't have, it was not kind. Let's see why it happened (Teacher or Parent: State the truth without blaming).

> **Process:** *Talk directly to the person who was unkind to you. Tell your feelings.*

"Mike kicked me!" said John.

Teacher: "Please do not tell me, look at Mike and tell him how you felt when he kicked you."

"Mike you kicked me and I don't like it because it hurt me."

> **Process:** *Only the truth will work. Ask other person to answer with the truth.*

"John took my pencil so I kicked him," said Mike.

Teacher: "Please do not tell me, look at John and tell him how you felt when he took your pencil."

"John, I don't like it when you take my pencil. I cannot do my work and I don't like to get in trouble."

> **Process:** *Only the truth will work. Ask other person to answer with the truth.*

John said, "I took Mike's pencil because he pushed me in line this morning."

Teacher: "Please do not tell me, look at Mike and tell him how you felt when he pushed you.

"Mike, that hurt me this morning when you pushed me. I thought we were friends."

Process: *Only the truth will work. Ask other person to answer with the truth.*

"But Mrs. Bhaloo, I didn't push John. My shoe got caught in the rug and I fell forward. I didn't mean to push John."

Teacher: "Please do not tell me, look at John and tell him you didn't mean to push him"

"John, I didn't mean to push you. We are friends."

Process: *Use kind words.*

Teacher: "So, you were both angry all day because of something that happened this morning. Anger builds if you do not resolve issues as they come up. What could you both have done differently to have solved this conflict when it happened?"

Mike: "I could have told John I didn't mean to push him when it happened."

Teacher: "Is that all you would need to do to resolve the issue?"

Mike: "I could have said I'm sorry, but I didn't push him on purpose!"

Teacher: "Sometimes things just happen. We do not spend time blaming or defending. The choice is simple: would you like to travel on the path of peace or the difficult path?"

On the peace path, Mike would have said to John, "I'm sorry, I didn't mean to push you. You are my friend. Let's play together."

On the difficult path, Mike and John stay angry all day long. They fight and have hurt feelings. They have no one to play with and the day is long and difficult. Which path do you choose?

Mike: "I want to be on the peace path. It's more fun. I'm sorry, I did not mean to push you. Would you like to play?"

John: "No, I don't want to play today. I'm still hurt."

Tomorrow is another day

Let children know that they might have hurt feelings today, but tomorrow brings a new day and a new start. Negative feelings must be released or they will fester and grow. We would rather have the Love light shine instead.

Teacher: "Sometimes, we need a day to release our negative emotions. Remember, you can blow your negative feelings into a big bubble and release them."

John: "Mike you are my friend. I would like to play with you tomorrow, okay."

There can be no path to peace if we do not teach children how to resolve conflicts. It takes time and patience but the rewards are great. Children are empowered and can feel pride in the fact, that they, not the teacher, resolved the issue. Often, parents want to solve the issue quickly and take the process away from the children.

*Children feel self-confident when they have
the power to solve the conflict.
Teach your children the path to peace.*

Super Star Teachers
Carol Elias and Eleanor Jordan

Super Star teachers Eleanor Jordan (left) and Carol Elias (right), with Mayre in the middle—getting ready for a big school production.

Panic set in when Mayre was about to graduate from kindergarten. Mrs. Bhaloo has been such a Super Star teacher that Mayre was reading on a sixth grade level and doing 4-digit math in kindergarten. It wasn't just the academics I wanted for my daughter, I wanted the joy of learning. I wanted the peace curriculum to continue because it aligned with our family values.

The easiest and most cost effective thing to do would have been to enroll Mayre in the elementary public school that was within walking distance of my house. Believe me, as a past public schoolteacher, that is exactly what I wanted to do.

I went to the public school and I said, "My daughter Mayre will be entering first grade. She can read on a sixth grade level and do 4-digit math—may I ask, what can you do for her? " The answer, "We can let the other kids catch up to her. We have no advanced classes until third grade."

Perhaps the more appropriate answer could have been "How exciting you have a child who can read on such a high level—you must be so proud. Although we do not have an advanced curriculum until third grade, we will work with your child at the appropriate level. How did your child advance to this level? Did you work with her at home, or was it the pre-school she attended?"

The public school missed a golden opportunity to have an outstanding student and an encouraging parent attend their school. They missed a golden opportunity to discover how a student attained such a high level. They missed a golden opportunity to use that new information to help other teachers attain that level with their students. How unfortunate for the public school!

New Vistas Academy, a small private school had gotten rave reviews by everyone with whom I spoke. Founder and Co-Director, Carol Elias, started the school in 1979 because of her disillusionment with the public pre-school system. She had been teaching first grade and discovered that the pre-school children who had gone to public school had twice the bad habits and behavior problems as children who had never gone to school.

She and another teacher pooled their retirement money and opened the doors to New Vistas Academy. Their goals were simple: To encourage the growth of each student to fulfill their potential as positive, responsible, contributory and loving individuals—many of the same principles as our Montessori class. Signs lined the halls and the front office:

We practice random acts of kindness at New Vistas.

In the middle of difficulty, lies opportunity.
—Albert Einstein.

Yesterday is History.
Tomorrow is a Mystery.
Today is a Gift.
That's why we call it "The Present."

Mayre was immediately enrolled in first grade. Later, I asked Carol: What made you the teacher you are today? What lessons would you like to share with others so they, too, can raise Super Stars?

Carol warmly grinned, "I always wanted to be a teacher. I wanted to be a teacher and be in that classroom so badly that I completed college in two and one-half years instead of four."

She went on to say how fortunate she was to have had such wonderful mentors in education. She was greatly influenced by her Aunt Anna, a teacher for over 50 years. When her aunt was in her 90s, she was placed in a senior center. Carol went to visit her and rapped on her aunt's door. Carol asked if she might come in for a visit. Her aunt replied, "Not right now dear, I'm in the middle of class and my students need me. I'll be with you when class is over."

What a great validation for teaching! Her aunt had gone back to the happiest time in her life, teaching—if only in her memory.

Carol and her Co-Director, Dr. Eleanor Jordan, who joined New Vistas in 1995, wanted to share their suggestions to ensure school success for your Super Star.

Align Preschool with Your Family Values

Preschool years are very important. Be sure the preschool you choose reflects your long-range plans for your child's education. Expectations begun in preschool last a lifetime. Use the ideas from this book to select the proper learning environment for your child.

Set Aside Home Time to Support Schoolwork and Homework

What you as a parent support, your child will support. Set aside home time to support schoolwork. This helps the child understand that you value education.

☆ **Help your child set up a bulletin board** or some type of home system to remember what needs to be returned to school each day.

☆ **Assist your child in returning the items at first.** Then turn responsibility over to your child. Just by creating a system, you send a clear signal to your child that it is important to return school assignments on time.

☆ **Return parental notes on time** to model positive behavior for your child.

☆ **Set aside a place at home to do schoolwork.** Make sure you have a supply box with pencils, markers, paper, etc. readily available.

☆ **Spot-check your child's homework periodically.** Sit down with your child to talk about homework. Talking about interesting aspects of an assignment helps your child develop enthusiasm and helps your child see you as a part of the educational team.

☆ **Make homework a priority.** Homework before everything else. Complete homework before sports, social activities and TV. It will set up a positive lifelong learning habit!

Empower Your Child

Let your child accept responsibility for his or her homework. Try not to make excuses to the teacher for your child's lack of preparedness. Children easily pick up your attitudes and behaviors and learn to make excuses too. Teach your children to take responsibility by giving them only two possibilities:

1. I did the homework. I am proud I completed my assignments.
2. I did not do the homework. It was my responsibility. I accept the consequences.

☆ **Help your child learn to communicate his or her needs to the teacher.** Encourage your child to talk directly with the teacher about assignments. If your child needs help, encourage her or him to ask the teacher for help with the assignment or anything surrounding the assignment.

☆ **If you and your child attend a conference, make sure your child is the one who expresses a concern that might have been expressed to you at home.** Encourage your child to write down any concerns prior to the conference. At the appropriate time, have your child bring up the concerns with the teacher. Effective communication helps your child develop future problem solving skills.

☆ **Teach your child that good manners help with effective communication.** It is amazing how often good manners will get a child through a stressful social situation and how these manners color people's opinions of your child. Manners help in dealing with peers, teachers, and parents. It also helps your child be less self-centered and think of others.

Attendance Is Important

Attendance in school is very important. Students who rarely miss school usually have fewer social problems and are generally in the "top" class groups.

☆ **Encourage your child to work through minor illnesses.**
Always giving in to illness gives the power to the illness.
Habits begun with health during childhood last a lifetime. To encourage working through minor illnesses,
one parent cleverly informed her child:

> *Sick children need their rest. When you are sick, I*
> *want you to get well fast. Our house rule is . . . If*
> *you are sick enough to stay home from school, then*
> *you are sick. Therefore, you must stay in bed all day.*
> *Your feet should not touch the floor for anything but*
> *bathroom breaks. Reading and TV would hurt your*
> *eyes, so there will be no TV. Games would not*
> *provide you with the proper rest, so there will be no*
> *games. You may do nothing but sleep all day.*

This parent said, "This rule cuts down on all the fake
illnesses, if you are willing to be consistent with it. My
children would rather go to school than to stay in bed all day
being bored."

Compete with Yourself

Competing with oneself is powerful. Competing with others
places the power in them. Encourage your child to strive to
be the best he or she can be. Encourage your child to com-
pete with his or her own work, not with others. Explore how
your child could improve grades, improve self-esteem, improve assignments, or improve test-taking ability.

Communicate Effectively with Your Child's Teacher

Schools should be held accountable for your child's learning. Effective communication between parents and teachers
is most important. When teachers and parents partner to
help children become Super Stars, the results are lots of
Super Stars.

Begin each parent teacher communication with the
premise:

What can we do together to help this child become the Super Star he or she deserves to be?

Blaming, attacking, and accusing are not effective communication tools for anyone. Sharing, discussing and suggesting are much more effective in helping to assess the challenge.

☆ **Never let your child feel your concerns until you have a plan to help correct them.** If you have concerns about things that might be happening in the classroom, talk it over with the teacher or administrator at your child's school. We often worry children needlessly about a concern we might have. After talking it over with the teacher or administrator, it might be easily solved. Your child, however, might hang on to the worries long after the problem has been corrected.

☆ **Ask for testing to assess your child's ability and achievement** if a teacher does not have a clear picture of your child's ability.

☆ **Ask the teacher to be very specific.** If the teacher suggests your child is struggling with a concept or subject— ask for specifics. What are the concepts or skills that are causing difficulty? Then ask the teacher to show you how she or he teaches that skill, in the class, so you can help your child, at home, using the same terminology.

☆ **If you feel your child is not being challenged in an important subject area—**bring it up to the teacher and/or the administrator. Ask for suggestions on how to work together to make the work more challenging.

☆ **Tell the teacher the things that she or he does that you do like.** This helps the teacher put your suggestions or complaints in perspective. Your child will be more apt to be positive about the classroom activities if he or she hears you compliment the teacher.

Service to Others

Helping others lends power to our own lives. Give your children opportunities to experience the joy of helping. Talk about current events and show your children how very fortunate we are to live in America.

Every child is special in some way. Every child has the potential to be a Super Star! We, as adults, must work together to provide our children with many opportunities to acquire the necessary skills to develop their talents. Offer encouragement and model the behavior and attitudes you want to see increase in your child. Together we can create Super Stars!

Insights and Notes

19

The Importance of Role Models

Super Star Role Model
Nancy Lieberman-Cline

On Labor Day, Mayre and I went to a neighborhood pool party. Mayre was having a blast with a lady named Nancy as they raced in the pool on huge inflatable toys. When the children got out of the pool, they gathered around Nancy as she told them her story.

I'm from New York City, and we didn't have big swimming pools like this one. We played in the streets with only a ball. As a girl, I loved sports—especially basketball. Basketball got me out of the house, and when I played basketball, I felt free. I quickly found out that if I played ball with the boys, I could PLAY the game instead of standing on the sidelines with the other girls cheering. I liked playing the game. Sports made me feel really good about myself.

But, back then, if a girl loved sports they teased her by calling her "tomboy." My mother was not very encouraging either and she kept saying, "Girls don't play sports, It's not lady like." When I asked, "Why?" she would just say, "They just don't play sports." So I

Nancy Lieberman-Cline helping Mayre learn to spin the basketball on her finger. Look out Harlem Globetrotters!

proclaimed "Yeah? I'll show you. I'll make history one day!"

Can you imagine, there were no woman sports heroes like there are today? All my role models were guys. Muhammad Ali was the greatest athlete overall in my eyes. He was everything I wanted to be—bold, brash, and confident. Some people thought he was cocky because he always said, "I am the Greatest!" But to me it wasn't cocky, because he could do what he said he could do. Ali backed up everything he said. He was the greatest!

My basketball heroes were Willis Reed and Walt Frazier. Willis Reed had great leadership qualities and a lot of determination. He was the team captain who held the Knicks together. Walt Frazier was cool, calm, and determined. He was always patient, and it paid off when he would come up with a timely steal and basket. The Knicks had the city wrapped around their little fingers and I hoped, someday, I would be the toast of a town, too.

I watched my heroes on TV every chance I got. Then I would go out in the schoolyard and practice every move I had seen Reed or Frazier make on TV. I practiced for hours and had fantasy games with my heroes. I even wore the jersey number 10 because Frazier did. I created shots and dreamed that I was beating all the other NBA stars.

Nothing got in the way of my dream to play basketball. Every time someone teased me, it made me work harder and practice harder to prove them wrong. My mother couldn't afford to help me, so I had a paper route to make money to buy my basketball shoes and equipment. I wanted to play basketball so much I even took a train, every night, by myself, to Harlem. I would be the only girl to play at Rutger's Park, with all guys—mostly black— because they were the best. I wanted to play with the best. I never stopped working, wanting, and dreaming.

> *I'm grateful to basketball because it taught me to be strong. It taught me how to win and lose, how to be well rounded, and how to lead. It made me successful because I believed in myself, worked hard every day, and had God in my corner. When I was on the Olympic platform, with the medal around my neck and the American flag waving before me, I knew I wanted to help young people, especially girls, know that dreams can come true. My motto was and is, "Never stop working, wanting, or dreaming."*

All the while Nancy talked, she was showing the kids how to control the basketball. Nancy's love of children emanated from her, and Mayre, like the other children, were mesmerized. Mayre, who is usually intimidated with balls of any type—basketball, softball, or volleyball—begged Nancy to show her a basketball trick. Nancy took Mayre's finger and twirled the basketball on it. Mayre was so proud of herself and yelled, "Mother come look what I can do!"

This incredible woman, who took the time to teach a group of eager children how to be Super Stars, was Nancy Lieberman-Cline, one of the most accomplished and recognized individuals in the history of women's basketball, for that matter, in the history of women's sports. Nancy instantly became a role model for my daughter as she has been for thousands of other little children worldwide.

Nancy could have boasted about her long and successful career:

☆ The youngest basketball player in Olympic history to win a medal as the United States captured the Silver under the direction of women's basketball legend Billie Moore.

☆ The first woman ever to play in a men's professional league where she met her husband Tim Cline. Marriage agreed with Nancy and she continued her meteor rise to Super Stardom.

☆ The first woman to be inducted into the New York City Basketball Hall of Fame, and later inducted into the Naismith Hall of Fame.

☆ Nancy was there, in 1997, for the birth of The Women's National Basketball Association, as the oldest player (38) in the league, playing for the Phoenix Mercury.

☆ Nancy was recruited to build a premier WNBA franchise in Detroit as General Manager and Head Coach. She led the second year Detroit Shock into the WNBA play-offs.

☆ Nancy's multi-faceted basketball acumen includes a wealth of athletic accomplishments, an extensive broadcasting career, successful business ventures, and generous community involvement. She has donated much of her time to various charities, including Special Olympics, Juvenile Diabetes, and Girl Scouts.

☆ She developed a scholarship program especially for girls to help build confidence and self-esteem by becoming involved in sports. Nancy believes, "You aren't on a level playing field with men unless you play sports. Basketball has taught me so much: How to win and how to lose, how to share information, and how to lead. Skills that you just can't get off the field."

Nancy's passion for basketball made her a Super Star athlete. But her passion for kids has made her a Super Star Role Model. Nancy's biggest accomplishment has been the birth of her only son Timothy Joseph, Jr. (TJ).

I asked Nancy: "What lessons would you like to share with others so they, too, can raise Super Stars?

Techniques and Attitudes

Be committed. You must be committed to be there for your child. Even though Nancy travels, her son, TJ, goes with her as often as possible. In his first five years, TJ made over 200 flights and met such notables as Michael Jordan, Kevin Costner, Billie Jean King, and Martina Navratilova. When Nancy played for the Phoenix Mercury, TJ was right there at every practice. Nancy and husband, Tim, both model the values their family supports—hard work and a passion for what they love, basketball. They also believe they have been blessed and give back by supporting Special Olympics, Juvenile Diabetes, and the Girl Scouts. When Nancy or Tim must be away from TJ, they have a "game board" to show TJ when they will return, "Mom will be back home in this many sleeps (meaning nights away)." This helps TJ understand the concept of time and assures him Mom will return.

Develop special talents by setting and attaining big goals. Nancy observed TJ's special talents and encouraged them. When TJ was five, Nancy noticed that he had the same talent his dad has—a wonderful grasp of numbers, statistics and great recall. TJ would plead for her to read him the NBA standings. She used this talent to help him in school. To encourage TJ to behave in class, she made a board to duplicate the NBA standings board. If TJ brought home a smiley face from school, it was put on the board:

1 Smiley Face to 0 Frowny Faces
A 1 and 0 Standing

TJ had to be over 500 to make the Family Play Offs. Because it was fun and a goal he could achieve, TJ worked hard to make the Family Play Offs.

Create a winning atmosphere. Nancy plays nerf basketball in the foyer of their home. Nancy gives TJ basketball number problems such as: If Mom makes a pull up jumper for 2 points, then she makes a 3 point shot, and goes one and one from the foul line, how many points did Mom make?

Nancy names the 12 teams in the WNBA. TJ must then go to the map and find the 12 cities for these teams. TJ also knows all 50 WNBA cards and can recall each woman's name and number on their jersey.

TJ is experiencing many small successes at an early age. Nancy has created a winning atmosphere so TJ will develop the confidence to achieve in many areas: TJ is a Super Star.

Nancy's belief in hard work and persistence paid off for her. Nancy knocked down the doors of prejudice and led the way for all women athletes of today.

Nancy's ability to encourage young people has also paid off. Many children, around the world, are on their way to becoming Super Stars thanks to a woman with a dream and a belief she could make it come true—Nancy Lieberman-Cline.

Nancy and Mayre having a good time.

20

 **Health**

The first six years Mayre was in the U.S.A. she had health problems. After the surgeries to repair her cleft palate and hearing loss, she continued to have a constant runny nose. No matter what I did, I could not prevent this. I used to cringe when she sneezed because the stuff that flew out of her nose made me lose my cookies on more than one occasion.

Each and every month she had a sinus infection, allergy problem or cold. Mayre would bring this cold home and the next day I was sick. We passed a different "bug" back and forth monthly, which meant doctor visits for the two of us.

Each doctor would give us antibiotics. One physician suggested Mayre and I had asthma and put us on inhalers. Another suggested a three-month regimen of antibiotics for Mayre to clear the runny nose. Well, I'm no doctor but I did not want to continue putting Mayre, or myself, on antibiotics.

The Search for Solutions

My quest to find a solution to our health challenges began, and I went to health food stores, homeopathic seminars, and listened to friends. Then the answer presented itself. A company named Arbonne engaged me to speak in Dallas. To customize my speeches, I always research the company. I read the following about Arbonne.

☆ Peter Morck the founder, had a vision, "I want people to look great and feel great by incorporating premium products based on herbal and botanical ingredients into their daily lives. Arbonne products are all about your overall health and wellness."

☆ Arbonne products are formulated in Switzerland and made in the U.S.A.

☆ The Premium skin care products have proprietary formulas that are:
Botanically-based
pH correct
hypoallergenic
dermatologist tested
never tested on animals
formulated without animal products or by-products
formulated without MINERAL OILS and
formulated without dyes or chemical fragrances.

☆ Arbonne expanded into total body care with nutrition products (vitamins and antioxidants) weight management, fitness and life enhancement products which are convenient, safe, backed by the latest scientific research and are formulated:
Using the finest pharmaceutical grade ingredients
To provide maximum absorption with highly
bio-available ingredients
Using Standardized botanicals and herbs
Without colors, starch, yeast, caffeine, preservatives or salt
Using proprietary herbal blends that work
synergistically with active components for
optimal results.

I was impressed by their literature, but it was the Arbonne audience that made me think about trying these products. They were one of the most enjoyable groups I have ever spoken before. They gave back so much energy.

When I got home I was compelled to try some of these products. Since I have been plagued with eczema, both on my face and body, I tried the skin care products first. Within one week my eczema was gone. Four years of dermatologists to no avail, and one week on Arbonne and my skin was clear. Naturally, I became a believer. I then tried the children's chewable vitamins on Mayre and the adult antioxidants on myself. We had nothing to lose and everything to gain.

My allergies cleared up immediately so, being the adult, I stopped taking the product because I was cured. Mayre, on

Maureen and Mayre (age 3) out for a run in the park.

the other hand, thought they were candy and took them for an entire month. At the end of the month, Mayre came to me and said, "Mother, please do not let me run out of these children's chewables." I replied, "Why?" She shook her head and said, "You didn't even notice my nose is not running! It's the first time the other kids did not call me snot nose."

Tears formed in my eyes and I was devastated. I had no idea the other children were teasing my baby over a runny nose that we hadn't been able to control until now. Immediately, I called for a three months supply. I asked why these antioxidants were so good. I learned they contained:

> *Green tea for overall good health, grape seed extract which has one of the highest levels of antioxidant activity recorded, and is fabulous for sinus and allergy problems and, a proprietary blend of broccoli, cabbage, tomato, carrots, spinach, and others.*

Great way to get Mayre to eat her veggies. In three months we did not have one doctor visit.

We have now been on Arbonne products for over two years and have not had a return doctor visit since. We have saved a ton of money and take no sinus medications or inhalers. My doctor called just recently wondering why we had not been in to see her in so long. She then answered her own question with, "It's those Arbonne Antioxidants that you and Mayre take, isn't it?"

Get Healthy

Find a good antioxidant and multivitamin supplement for you and your Super Star

Recently I heard a public health commercial that stated the number one reason children are absent from school is asthma related health problems. We need to have our children on good supplements to augment their diets.

To prevent one child from being teased about a runny nose, I will gladly share Arbonne information with you. Also, the nutrition bars have been great for Mayre's lunches.

Research the nutritional products on the market and make sure your Super Star is on one. It is very difficult to be a smashing success when you are sick and tired all the time.

For more information about Arbonne products call me at (800)485-0065 or if you live in Arizona (480)759-6251, Fax (480)759-6257, or e-mail mgmul@aol.com.

Make Sure Your Super Star Gets Plenty of Rest

Children need at least 8 to 12 hours of sleep every night just to maintain. I have had many a parent complain that their child stays up until all hours of the night. Parents must take a leadership role. To maintain health, you and your child must get the proper rest. Many issues are negotiable, but health issues and safety issues are not. Parents must be Parents.

Set appropriate bedtimes and stick to it

Be consistent. Do not put your child to bed at 8 p.m. one night and 10 p.m. the next night. Set appropriate bedtimes. It took a month of consistency to get Mayre on an appropriate schedule. In Vietnam she had gone to bed at sun down and awakened at sun up. When she got to the U.S.A., she wanted to stay up with Mom. Consistency is the key—create a night time routine. Just starting the routine signals bedtime is near.

Practice the routine in the day time so they know what to do at bedtime

Put on pajamas, brush teeth, get drink, go potty, say prayers, get in bed, go to sleep. Don't forget the last one—Go to sleep.

Mayre, can you show me all the things we do to get ready for bed? Once you get in bed can you get up and come back out? NO ... that is correct ... You are well prepared for bedtime. Now let's switch ... you be the mom and I'll be the kid. Great. Let's practice again.

Let your Super Star tell you the reasons why she does not need to come back out. Let your Super Star tell you why she must go to bed at a certain time.

Then put your child to bed.

If she gets up for any reason—drink , potty, whatever— put her back in her bed. "It is bedtime now. Tomorrow we will practice again."

Exercise Is Vital

Today's children do not get as much exercise as they should. They have a lack of freedom to go to the parks, tight time schedules and sedentary lifestyles. With diabetes and other diseases on the rise, we must put exercise back into our schedules. I go to a personal trainer twice a week to model proper exercise for Mayre. If we can walk or ride bikes to get to our destination, we walk rather than take the car. If we go shopping, we park as far from the entrance as possible, so we at least have to walk to the store. We ride our bikes to nearby stores on the weekend.

Model the healthy lifestyle and your Super Star will follow.

Insights and Notes

21

⭐ Kind-Heartedness

We are such a bountiful nation. We have so much. We much teach our children to be thankful and to be generous in service and sympathetic toward the needy and unfortunate as the poem "Character" states.

While in Vietnam, I discovered the main concern the Vietnamese have for Americans adopting their children is that we have too much. They feared Mayre would not learn to share and serve her fellow humans. I assured them that our Mulvaney family valued generous service to others. I promised to teach Mayre how to be of service to others.

SHOW THANKFULNESS

Acknowledge everything
and be thankful for everything

Make mealtime, car time, or exercise, a time to express thanks—out loud—for your blessings. We start our meals with a prayer, and then everyone is asked to express their thanks for something that happened that day. On the short drive to school, we have a certain spot, every day where we take time to express our thanks. Take time to be thankful.

Create Service Time

Each time Mayre outgrew her toys and clothes, I wanted to make a time to take those items to be given away. Most of the charities in our area have trucks that come and pick up the items, but that would not have given us service time. I wanted Mayre to give her things away in person.

Do you know how difficult that is in today's society? I phoned 15 charities that would not allow us to donate, person to person. Every agency would gladly come pick up the items but because of security issues would not let us donate directly. Finally, I found a charity that would let us donate person to person. If I had given up and let the truck pick up the items, Mayre would never have known the joy of giving away something she valued. She would have missed the smile of thanks from the other child.

One year we even adopted a family and went to their home to celebrate each set of donations. We then started involving others in this so they, too, could experience the joy of giving.

Another favorite way to serve is to go to a senior citizen nursing home. A friend's father was placed in a nursing home after heart surgery, and we went to visit. Mayre had the opportunity to serve the seniors by helping them exercise. She would place a ball by their foot and say, "The therapist said you are supposed to kick the ball. I'll go get it if you will kick it." or "You are supposed to toss the ring over the mark. I'll catch for you if you will toss it here." By the end of the session, everyone was laughing. Mayre felt the joy of helping.

You cannot just tell your Super Stars to help others, you must create situations where they physically are able to help.

Whether you volunteer to pick up trash along the side of the highway, volunteer for the Special Olympics, or send money to people devastated by the hurricanes—seek out opportunities to allow your children to feel the joy of service! Helping others develops the Super Star value of Kind-heartedness.

Exercise

Make a list of ways your family could be of service to others or to your community.

Then ask each child in your family to add to that list.

Insights and Notes

22

Visualize Being
A Super Star

All my life I had loved to run, but when I started entering 10k races in El Paso, Texas, I experienced extensive pain after only a mile. I thought I was just being a wimp so I continued to run. A monster race, called the Trans-Mountain was announced at the 10K I just completed. Thousands of runners competed. The race consisted of running up one side of the mountain six miles and going down the back side for another five miles. I trained every day, in pain, because I was determined to run this Trans-Mountain race.

VISUALIZATION IS A POWERFUL TOOL

Each day, for two months, I visualized exactly what I would wear for the race—the shorts, the jersey, and the shoes. I visualized the crowd cheering me on. I visualized coming across the finish line with my hands high in the air in victory. I made an image book of me running in this race. I looked at those pictures daily.

Although I ran in 10k races weekly, I usually finished at the end. I was content to be what the newspaper called, "The jolly jogger! MGM finishes near the end of the race but she always has a great big smile and encourages the other racers." The pain was always intense, so I was slow but steady. I just wanted to finish the race.

The day of the Trans-Mountain I was ready and anxious to begin. I looked like a winner and I felt like a winner. The race began. I dropped to the back of the pack as the pain was unbelievable. At one point the pain became so intense that I sat right down on the pavement in the middle of all the runners. It felt like I was running on two bricks.

Then something happened. The crowd cheered me on saying, "Don't give up! You can do it!" I had visualized myself in this race with the crowd cheering me. I had seen myself coming over the mountain and down to the finish line. I had seen myself crossing the finish line in victory. I had to get up.

I got up and limped up the mountain. I was slow but moving forward. At the top of the mountain, I noticed there were only two people left in the race—a male runner and myself. Everyone else had finished the race and was at the bottom celebrating. I was determined to finish this race if it killed me.

I pulled ahead of the male racer, at a snail pace, but ahead. He gritted his teeth and limped ahead of me. All of a sudden the people at the bottom of the hill began to look up to the mountain. They were watching these two fools limping back and forth around each other. They began to cheer. I began to pick up steam. I forgot the pain and charged ahead.

By the time we got down the mountain, the other runners held up a finish line. It was exactly like I had visualized. I broke into a full trot and poured it on. I ran like the energizer bunny on speed. I put my hands up and crossed the finish line in victory beating the male runner. I was overjoyed!

Although I had finished next to last, I had finished just the way I had visualized—breaking the finish line tape, hands up in victory.

Visualization is so important to teach your Super Star. You can have anything you want if you will visualize and work toward our goals.

Put It in Pictures

Every year Mayre makes a image book or an image poster. She focuses on what she would like to be in different areas of her life:

Health	Happiness
Prosperity	Service
School	Career
Music	Family
Friends	Spiritual

We then sit and cut out pictures from magazines to create the picture of what she would like to become. It becomes a collage, or you can make a page for each section—a health page etc. Mayre puts a picture of herself over the face of the pictures from the magazines. (We usually have an abundance of the little stick on pictures from school.) We place these pictures on the mirror in the bathroom so she sees them daily.

Set Positive, Specific, Attainable Goals—IN WRITING.

Mayre writes her goals on 3x5 cards. We place the cards strategically about the house so she sees them often. Since the mind does not know the difference between reality and what it sees daily, Mayre becomes what she sees daily.

There is magic in writing down your goals. Please do not forget to let your child include financial or prosperity goals. I am always amazed that we do not teach our children about finances. We will talk about any subject expect money. I do not remember one teacher mentioning how to make money, how to spend money, how to keep track of money, or how to give money away. Nothing. Even my parents, who had a wonderful outlook on finances, never talked about it. Is it any wonder we are a nation in debt?

Talk to your children about money. Teach them the value of money—the joy of giving away money when you have enough. Give them your closed old checkbooks to practice with. Have them write you a check for an IOU. Teach them the joy of earning money. Mayre helps to make our bank deposits, she is involved in an investment plan where she helps choose the investments after researching them, and she has a bank account. If you never talk about money, your children never learn to take control of their own financial well being.

Positive Affirmations

Have your children affirm the positive qualities about themselves. Let them write down the positive facts about their lives. What you see, you believe.

Start with:	I AM or I Mayre (your name of course).
Make it positive,	I am a bright student.
Make it in the present tense	I am a happy child. (Not I would someday like to be happy—but I am happy now!)
Make it about you, not the other person	I am an effective Parent.
Be realistic but stretch	I am a Super Star Student!

Children will have enough negativity out in the world. They will often hear, in school and other places, 15 negatives for every positive. Do not be afraid your children will become conceited by saying positive self-statements. Know that they will become self-assured. You cannot give away what you do not have. Children, like adults, will never be able to share with others and encourage others if they will not encourage themselves. Teach them self-assurance.

Healthy—I am healthy. I love to eat healthy foods. I walk instead of ride.

Happy—I love mornings. I love sunsets. I love being alive. I am thankful and joyous.

Self-Assured—I am a Super Star Math wizard. I play the piano with enthusiasm and joy. People like to hear me play. I am self-confident.

Bright—I love to learn. Reading makes me happy. I am a bright student.

Kind-Hearted—I feel warm inside when I help others. I seek opportunities to serve others.

Loving—I love my family and my family loves me. I am free from sharp words. I encourage my family team members.

"Bonker's Free"— I am calm and peaceful. I enjoy challenges. I am a good problem solver.

The moment I adopted Mayre, we started doing visualization exercises. We made the image books and started the writing exercises as soon as she could write.

It has been extremely powerful to help her become a
   Healthy,
      Happy,
         Self-Assured,
            Bright,
               Kind-Hearted,
               Loving,
                  "Bonker's Free"
                    Super Star.

MAYRE'S GOALS
8 YEARS OLD

My mother and I did a project and she told me that if I can see my goals I can make my goals come true.

This paper will tell all my goals.

SCHOOL

In school I will be good in math, use bright ideas, and be smart enough to go to Notre Dame College. I will get a scholarship for being smart. I will get all A's on my report card.

HEALTH

I want to be healthy. I exercise to stay strong. I eat fruits and veggies and stay away from sweets.

What I Want to Have

I want to be rich so I can take my family places, buy them things, make my life successful! I want my family to have fun. I'd like to have a vacation in a snowy place.

INVESTMENT AND MONEY

In my investment situation I want to invest in Disney. I will be rich enough to buy a van and a dog. I also want to be rich in love.

LIFE & CAREER

In my life I want to be a musician and a family doctor. When everyone sees me they'll say, "There's Little MGM the musician and loving, kindhearted doctor. I want to be just like her!" My little MGM will be my assistant like I am to my mother.

MAYRE'S CAREER GOALS

My goals are to become a rich, champion, famous, family doctor and musician. Since I have talent I'd like to be famous in Holly Wood. I want to be famous so I can meet Alicia Silverstone.

I made the poster on the next page to help me visualize my goals.

Mayre, practicing that Hollywood Super-Star Look.

23

☆ Any Kid Can Be A Super Star

Not all kids start out in life on equal footing. Some children, like my daughter Mayre, started life in abject poverty. There was little food, no medicine, and she had a cleft palate, hearing loss, and respiratory disease. Some considered Mayre a "throw away child." I just considered Mayre a "Super Star." My attitude was that any kid can be a Super Star because my definition was so simple:

A SUPER STAR IS A KID WHO IS
Healthy, Happy, Self-Assured, Bright,
Kind-Hearted, Loving, and "Bonker's Free."

To this day, I am thankful to a student named David who taught me that any kid can be a Super Star.

David had been in school for five years. He was in the fifth grade, but because he was such a discipline problem, they placed him in my special education class. The first day of class, David arrived in an agitated and angry state. He hit every kid in the class saying, "Get out my way." He then turned his wrath on me with a quick, "I hate you!" even though this was our first meeting. David flopped into his seat and began to disrupt the class by cussing and fussing.

He used four letter words that I had never even heard before. This behavior went on for the entire week.

At first, I suspected his behavior was a reaction to being placed in the special education class. Most kids would rather be labeled class clown or bully by peers than to be labeled stupid. After careful observation, I suspected there was more to the story. I decided to ask the other teachers, who had previously had David, what were his challenges.

Every teacher who had previously taught David told me he was a handful. Not one teacher said a kind thing about David. They told me it was a good thing I had lost my sense of smell because David literally stunk. The other children complained about sitting next to David so, most of the time, he was moved to the side, by himself.

I decided I should observe exactly what happened to David each and every day he came to school. Knowing that the first experience of the day is the most significant, I went out to the buses to watch David come into school. David had not even gotten off the bus before the bus driver yelled at him. The two teachers on bus duty also yelled, "Slow Down David, Walk Young MAN!"

David raced to the lunchroom for his free breakfast. As David went down the line, he gobbled up everything in his path. The lunchroom staff yelled at him, "Don't eat like a little pig, wait till you sit down!" David had the breakfast gone before he sat down and started begging the other kids for their left-overs.

David had three more unpleasant encounters with administrators and teachers before he finally arrived in our wing. Then the children began to taunt him. "Here comes Stink Boy," or "I smell something, it must be stinky David."

I don't know about you, but when I receive poor service, it makes me angry. I started to think David had received poor customer service from every staff member in the school. He was angry about the treatment he received each and every day he came to school. I knew I had to do something about David. Children cannot learn when they are hungry and smelly. I needed to talk to David parents. They apparently did not care about him, and I needed to give them a piece of my mind.

Of course, the other teachers said, "Good Luck. David's parents have never once come in to school even though they have eight children who have gone here. We have sent note after note and they will not come in."

I would have to go to David's parents. The other teachers said, "Are you crazy! You cannot do that. Let the social services people take care of the problem. It isn't safe to go out there." Nothing they said could dissuade me.

I told David to tell his father I would be out to visit him in the afternoon. David said, "You come out to my house Ms. Olevaney (his nick name for me) and them dogs will eat your chicken legs right off." I replied, "Well David, you tell your daddy I'll be out there and I'll bring my chicken legs with me."

David lived in a very rural part of Maryland and his house was surrounded by tobacco farms. The directions were, "Now, you go down that dirt road to the second house, then you turn until you see the car in the front yard, go past that and turn into the next driveway. You'll hear the dogs."

When I finally pulled up in front of David's house, my mouth fell open. David and all his brothers and sisters were lined up on the porch, quiet and well-behaved. The house was about to tip over—or so it appeared. It was completely slanted at a 90 degree angle. There was no running water and no bathroom facilities. The grandmother was standing in the doorway, the mother was locked in a car because she had just been released from a mental institution and the authorities were afraid she would hurt herself or one of the kids. The father was standing at the bottom of the stairs waiting for me.

This was the most humbling experience of my life. I had come there, ready to do battle with this family that apparently did not care, and all I saw was a man trying to do the best he could. I changed my attitude immediately. I asked permission to bring my "chicken legs" on his property, and I asked if he would be so kind to hold the dogs back.

I said, "Sir, I would like to tell you about your son David. I believe he is one of the most unique students I have ever had." Now, that was not a lie—he was unique. I went on, "I believe your son is very smart, but it seems he is receiving very poor customer service at our school. I would like to help him if I may."

"Ms. Mulvaney" said the father, "You do anything you want to help my David. No teacher ever come out to tell me they wanted to help. They send me these papers, but I don't read so good. I tries, as best I can. I don't got any help 'cept my mother and she ain't doin' too good herself."

"Sir, I see you do not have any running water. We have running water at the school. Would it be alright if I let your son David take a shower every day?"

"Yes, mam, that be okay."

"We have a washing machine at school. Would it be alright if I let David wash his clothes every day?"

"Yes, mam, that be okay. Whatever you want to do with my David, you do. You hear that boy!"

"Sir, I am proud and honored you took the time out of your busy schedule to talk to me today. I hope I did not keep you from your work. I will do everything I can to help your child."

"Nobody ever been that kind. My son David is a super kid. With a little help, I knows he can be a Super Star!"

That meeting with David's father was the most life-changing experience I had ever had. I was taken aback that a man with a third grade education had more insight than a whole school of supposedly educated teachers. David had been in the school for five years and not one person had ever dared to find out about him. He was passed from teacher to teacher and class to class like a bad rumor. No one ever got close enough to see the Super Star under all the dirt, except his father, who I foolishly thought didn't care. I was so wrong.

The next day, David bypassed the teachers at the bus. He even bypassed the free breakfast—which he so loved—and bypassed the children who taunted him. David came racing into my classroom screaming, "You better watch out or Ms. Olevaney will find your house. She'll find your house and she'll tell your daddy you is a Super Star. I ain't stinky no more—I am a Super Star!"

From that moment on, David was a changed child and I was a changed teacher. The student so often becomes the teacher, and I learned so much from my experience with David and his family. David's dad taught me to look for the Super Star in all my students. He taught me to change my attitude—ALL CHILDREN, STINKY OR NOT, ARE SUPER STARS. See each child as a super star and they will become super stars.

Immediately, I saw David as a Super Star and taught him to see himself as a Super Star. I taught David how to take a shower, wash his clothes, and take care of his personal needs.

I went to the lunchroom and asked that the lunchroom staff to make David a lunch to take home each evening so he would not be so hungry. I also asked that they send any extras home for the rest of the children. Then I asked them to change the way they addressed David and all the children in my class.

"From now on, when my class comes to the cafeteria, I would like you to say, 'Here comes the Super Stars!'" They agreed to do that for me.

In faculty meeting, I instructed the other staff members to please help me to increase the self-esteem of my students by addressing them as Super Stars for one solid month. They balked at first, but I told them it was for a new program I was using and I needed their assistance. I promised if they would help me, the behavior of my students would change dramatically in a positive way. They had noticed the change in David and readily agreed to help.

David's father loved his son and was a wonderful man, he just needed a little help from other positive adults to assist him. David needed role models that modeled positive adult behaviors.

David's behaviors changed, his subject levels went sky high, and David left my class that year with hope for a brighter future. He was the first member of his family to complete high school.

David needed someone to show him how to be a super star. David needed someone to expect him to be a super star. David then lived up to the expectation. David was a Super Star!

All children deserve to be Healthy, Happy, Self-Assured, Bright, Kind-Hearted, Loving, and "Bonker's Free" Super Stars.

Any kid can be a Super Star with the proper support from parents and the adult community.

☆ **Super Stars can be developed.** All it takes is a commitment on your part.

☆ **Commit to becoming the Best Parent you can Be or the Best Role Model you can Be.** Enjoy the Ride! Take your job as Parent or Role Model seriously, but don't take yourself seriously. Gain new information. If you did not like the way you were parented, change it. If you did like the way you were parented, improve on it.

☆ **Change your attitudes!** Forget "When I see it, I'll believe it!" Use the Attitude Technologies "When I believe it, I'll see it." When you believe All Kids Can Be Super

Stars you will see Super Star children! They will live up to your expectations.

☆ **Know your family values.** Talk about them frequently. Review your own family history. Write it down so you can see it clearly.

☆ **Make a strategic plan for your family.** Write the Plan down.

☆ **Plan to raise Super Stars**, don't expect it to happen just because you want it to.

☆ **Write your Family Vision.** Enlist the aid of all family team members. The vision is your picture of what you want your family to be.

☆ **Model your family values through your behaviors.** Ask others around you to assist in modeling positive adult behaviors. If others can't or won't help, double your efforts.

☆ **Define an action plan to support your Family Vision.** Use the strategies and techniques in this book to design your own action plan. Please do not dismiss the techniques because most of them were presented for younger children. I used these techniques on college students and they worked quite well. The techniques work—just make them viable for your particular age group.

☆ **Find role models to assist you on you mission.** Make sure all teachers, priests, preachers, friends, etc. are aligned with your Family Vision.

Make the choice to raise a Super Star! All kids deserve to be **Healthy, Happy, Self-Assured, Bright, Kind-Hearted, Loving, and "Bonker's Free" Super Stars.**

Appendix

BOOK LIST FOR LITERATURE BASED ETHICS CLASS

Author and Title	Subject
1. SOMETHING SPECIAL WITHIN Alice Jacobsen	Inner Peace
2. BLACK ELK SPEAKS — (Adult book; I reworded and condensed the book for the children)	Living the road of peace, not conflict
3. THE LEGEND OF THE BLUEBONNET Tomie DePaola	Compassion and Selflessness
4. THE ROSE AND THE PICKLE Adrienne Golday	Each person unique Words can hurt! Inner beauty is more important
5. NOBODY'S PERFECT, NOT EVEN MY MOTHER — Norma Simon	Using our mistakes as a learning tool
6. DON'T POP YOUR CORK ON MONDAYS Adolph Moser	Coping with stress
7. DON'T FEED THE MONSTER ON TUESDAY Adolph Moser	Child's self-esteem
8. ME FIRST AND THE GIMME GIMMES Gerald G. Jampolsky and Diane V. Cirincione	Blaming others for our problems Selfishness makes us unhappy
9. OUR PEACEFUL CLASSROOM Aline D. Wolf	Peaceful co-existence in a Montessori class
10. THE BALLAD OF THE HARP WEAVER Edna St. Vincent Millay	Empathy for others Joy of giving
11. ALL IS WELL Frank E. Peretti	Empathy for others
12. THE GIFT OF THE MAGI O'Henry	Be a giver, not a taker
13. THE GRINCH WHO STOLE CHRISTMAS Dr. Seuss	"Things" don't bring happiness

14. THE FISH KING'S POWER OF TRUTH;
   A JAKATA TALE
      Retold by Laura Mipham

15. BROTHER EAGLE, SISTER SKY   Love and take care
      A message from Chief Seattle   of the Earth

16. THE POWER OF A PROMISE;   Be true to our word
   A JAKATA TALE

17. THE ORPHAN BOY   Trust and
      Mollel Morin   truthfulness

18. FLUFFY AND SPARKY   A story of true
      Paula Elliott   friendship

19. KENJI AND THE MAGIC GEESE   Money and things
      Ryerson Johnson   don't make us
          truly happy

20. PEPITO'S STORY   It's alright to be
      Eugene Fern   different

21. KNOTS ON A COUNTING ROPE   We decide what's
      Bill Martin, Jr. & John Archambault   good or bad
          Having the courage
          to face a challenge

22. SADAKO AND THE THOUSAND   Sadness of war
   PAPER CRANES   Childhood illness
      Carol Heller and Elsie Williams
      Teaching Tolerance Magazine Spring '93

23. THE VALUE OF FRIENDS; A JAKATA TALE   Being a true friend

24. THE MAGIC OF PATIENCE; A JAKATA TALE   Success through
          patience

25. HEART OF GOLD; A JAKATA TALE   Kindness and
          compassion

26. KIDS; ANSWERS TO LIFE'S   Ethics and values
   BIG QUESTIONS
      Steve and Ruth Bennett

27. I CAN SAY NO, A CHILD'S BOOK ABOUT   Drug abuse
   DRUG ABUSE   education
      Doris Sanford

28. RACHAEL AND THE UPSIDE DOWN   Death of loved one
      A true story by Eileen Douglas (out of print)

29. PLEASE COME HOME   Children of divorce
      Doris Sanford

30. THE FALL OF FREDDIE THE LEAF   Death—a story of life
      Leo Buscaglia

MAUREEN G. MULVANEY
"A STAR SPEAKER" and A BIG PRODUCTION
for conventions, special events,
meetings and parenting workshops

If you are interested in engaging MGM as a speaker, Please call:

16026 S. 36th St. • Phoenix, AZ 85048-7322
(800) 485-0065 • (480) 759-6251 • Fax (480) 759-7257
e-mail: mgmul@aol.com

Or mail this form:

Name _____

Organization _____

Address_____

City/State/Zip _____

ARBONNE . . . THE NAME MIGHT BE NEW TO YOU BUT THE PRODUCTS <u>GET RESULTS</u>!

They've been around for 20 years.

- Ⓐ Arbonne products are PURE, SAFE & Beneficial
- Ⓐ Unparalleled in Quality & Effectiveness
- Ⓐ Based on Herbal and Botanical Swiss Formulations . . . Made in the U.S.A.

World-Class Reputation for Product Integrity

Ⓐ **SKIN CARE & COSMETICS**
Arbonne a Better Choice for your SKIN . . . Contains NO mineral oils, petroleum, SD40 alcohol, soap, acetone, collagen, dyes, perfumes, animal byproducts or harmful ingredients . . . less than 1% preservatives

Ⓐ **MULTI-VITAMINS & MINERAL SUPPLEMENTS**
(For Children, Teens, Women and Men)

Ⓐ **SPECIALIZED ANTIOXIDANTS**
(Contains Organic Vegetables, Green Tea, Grape Seed Extract, Beta Carotene, Vitamin C & E & more)

Ⓐ **LONGEVITY LINE**
(Varicose Veins, Men's Prostrate, Women's Menopause & PMS, Heart)

Ⓐ **FITNESS LINE**
(Joint Formula, Herbal Muscle Massage, BBP8 Complex, Optimal Performance Drink, Recovery Shake, Nutrition bars)

Call for more information :
Maureen G. Mulvaney
16026 S. 36th St. Phoenix, AZ 85048-7322
(800)485-0065 (480)759-6251 Fax (480) 757-6257
e-mail mgmul@aol.com

Get Started On Your Road To Good Health!

Mrs. Heidi Grimes
East Valley Yamaha Music School
3126 N. Arizona Ave. Suite 102
Chandler, AZ 85225
Phone: 480-926-4441   Fax: 480-926-4423
e-mail thgrimes@aol.com

Ahwatukee Foothills Montessori
3221 E. Chandler Blvd.
Phoenix, AZ 85044
Phone: 480-759-3810

New Vistas Academy
670 N. Arizona Avenue, Suite 35
Chandler, AZ 85225
Phone: 480-963-2313
e-mail CHTeachers@aol.com

Dr. Pepper
Nancy Lieberman - Clinic Basketball Camp
Presented by J.C. Penny
PO Box 795054
Dallas, TX 75379-5054
Phone: 972-612-6090
Basketball Camp for Girls age 7-17. Learn from an Olympian
Hall of Famer.